Oriens

ORIENS

A PILGRIMAGE THROUGH ADVENT AND CHRISTMAS

November 30, 2025–February 2, 2026

FR. JOEL SEMBER

Our Sunday Visitor
Huntington, Indiana

Nihil Obstat
Msgr. Michael Heintz, Ph.D.
Censor Librorum

Imprimatur
✠Kevin C. Rhoades
Bishop of Fort Wayne-South Bend
February 21, 2025

The *Nihil Obstat* and *Imprimatur* are official declarations that a book is free from doctrinal or moral error. It is not implied that those who have granted the *Nihil Obstat* and *Imprimatur* agree with the contents, opinions, or statements expressed.

Except where noted, the Scripture citations used in this work are taken from the *New American Bible*, revised edition © 2010, 1991, 1986, 1970 Confraternity of Christian Doctrine, Washington, D.C., and are used by permission of the copyright owner. All rights reserved. No part of the New American Bible may be reproduced in any form without permission in writing from the copyright owner.

Scripture citations marked "Lectionary" are taken from the *Lectionary for Mass for Use in the Dioceses of the United States*, second typical edition, Copyright © 2001, 1998, 1997, 1986, 1970 Confraternity of Christian Doctrine; Psalm refrain © 1968, 1981, 1997, International Committee on English in the Liturgy, Inc. All rights reserved. Neither this work nor any part of it may be reproduced, distributed, performed or displayed in any medium, including electronic or digital, without permission in writing from the copyright owner.

Excerpts from the English translation of *The Roman Missal* © 2010, International Commission on English in the Liturgy Corporation. All rights reserved.

Every reasonable effort has been made to determine copyright holders of excerpted materials and to secure permissions as needed. If any copyrighted materials have been inadvertently used in this work without proper credit being given in one form or another, please notify Our Sunday Visitor in writing so that future printings of this work may be corrected accordingly.

Copyright © 2025 Fr. Joel Sember
30 29 28 27 26 25   1 2 3 4 5 6 7 8 9

All rights reserved. With the exception of short excerpts for critical reviews, no part of this work may be reproduced or transmitted in any form or by any means whatsoever without permission from the publisher. For more information, visit: www.osv.com/permissions.

Our Sunday Visitor Publishing Division, Our Sunday Visitor, Inc., 200 Noll Plaza, Huntington, IN 46750; www.osv.com; 1-800-348-2440

ISBN: 978-1-63966-349-1 (Inventory No. T2982)
RELIGION—Holidays—Christmas & Advent.
RELIGION—Christian Living—Prayer.
RELIGION—Christianity—Catholic.
eISBN: 978-1-63966-350-7
LCCN: 2025935532

Cover design: Tyler Ottinger
Interior design: Amanda Falk

PRINTED IN THE UNITED STATES OF AMERICA

*Dedicated to my grandparents,
Milton and Marion and
Bill and Dorothy,
whose example of faith in God
and faithfulness to each other
continues to inspire me*

+

*and to all the faithful married couples who
have walked Oriens together*

+

¡Buen Camino!

WEEK 1
Sunday, November 30
ADVENT, 1ST SUNDAY

- Saturday, December 6 — SAINT NICHOLAS

WEEK 2
Sunday, December 7
ADVENT, 2ND SUNDAY

- Monday, December 8 — IMMACULATE CONCEPTION

- Friday, December 12 — OUR LADY OF GUADALUPE

WEEK 3
Sunday, December 14
ADVENT, 3RD SUNDAY

WEEK 4
Sunday, December 21
ADVENT, 4TH SUNDAY

- **Thursday, December 25 — NATIVITY OF OUR LORD**

WEEK 5
Sunday, December 28
HOLY FAMILY

- Thursday, January 1 — MARY, MOTHER OF GOD

WEEK 6
Sunday, January 4
EPIPHANY, OBSERVED

- Tuesday, January 6 — EPIPHANY

WEEK 7
Sunday, January 11
BAPTISM OF THE LORD

- Monday, January 12 — BAPTISM OF THE LORD

WEEK 8
Sunday, January 18
ORDINARY TIME, 2ND SUNDAY

WEEK 9
Sunday, January 25
ORDINARY TIME, 3RD SUNDAY

WEEK 10
Sunday, February 1
THE PRESENTATION OF THE LORD

- **Monday, February 2 — THE PRESENTATION OF THE LORD**

Contents

Introduction	9
Suggested Calendar for the Advent and Christmas Season	13
Blessing of an Advent Wreath	15
WEEK ONE (November 30–December 6)	19
Lectio Divina	21
WEEK TWO (December 7–13)	47
Imaginative Prayer	49
WEEK THREE (December 14–20)	79
The Secret to a Better Advent	81
WEEK FOUR (December 21–27)	115
Making Prayer Happen When You Get Busy	117
WEEK FIVE (December 28–January 3)	147
Well Begun Is Half Done	149
WEEK SIX (January 4–10)	175
Announcement of Easter and the Movable Feasts for the Year of Our Lord 2026	177
Blessing of the Home and Household on Epiphany	184
WEEK SEVEN (January 11–17)	205
Keep the Christmas Light Burning Brightly	207
WEEK EIGHT (January 18–24)	233
Discernment of Spirits	235

WEEK NINE (January 25–31)	267
Relational Prayer (ARRR)	269
WEEK TEN (February 1–2)	297
A Light to the Nations	299
Once a Pilgrim, Always a Pilgrim	312
Review of Reviews	313
Prayer Outlines	319

Introduction

Give a man a fish, and you feed him for a day.
Teach a man to pray, and you feed him for a lifetime.

TEACH A MAN TO PRAY ...

There are many wonderful Advent books full of moving meditations for you to choose from. This isn't one of them. Instead of giving you my meditations, this book will teach you how to meditate for yourself. If you don't really know how to pray with Scripture, this book will teach you. If you already know how to pray, then it will help you to pray better. I left space each day for you to journal your prayer experiences. When you get to the end of the book, you will find that it has become full of moving meditations, but they won't be my meditations; they'll be yours. I hope that, as you learn to go deeper in your conversations with God, prayer becomes your favorite part of each day, and this season takes on a whole new meaning.

IF YOU PRAYED WITH *ORIENS* BEFORE

You might be wondering how this book compares with previous editions. The format is exactly the same: We teach *lectio divina* and imaginative prayer, provide a Scripture passage each day, and give you space to journal. You will encounter familiar figures like John the Baptist, Zechariah and, of course, Mary and Joseph. Most of the Scripture passages are chosen to match with Lectionary Cycle A. *Oriens* 2025 will be like walking down a familiar road, but with new companions and at a new place in your life. If you've never done *Oriens* before, finish reading this introduction and then skim the rest of the introductory material through the first day (Sunday, November 30). That will give you a good sense of the road ahead.

"DO YOU WANT TO WALK THE CAMINO WITH ME?"

It was my third year of theology at the North American College in Rome.

We had two weeks of Easter vacation to go experience Europe. A classmate and I decided to walk the *Camino Portugués*, a shorter version of the famous medieval pilgrimage route across Spain. (It's so famous that it's called simply *El Camino*, which means "the way" in Spanish.) I bought some shoes and borrowed a backpack, and we flew to Lisbon. We took a train to the Portuguese border and spent a week walking to the burial place of St. James the apostle. Something special happened *on the way*. I started to see myself, and the ordinary world, in a whole new way. I discovered the magic of walking pilgrimages.

Three years later, I was back in America as a newly ordained priest. "We don't have to fly to Europe to walk down the road," I thought. I scoped out a walking route to a local shrine, lined up places to stay every twelve miles or so, and found people to bring us food each night. Twenty-two people joined me on that pilgrimage. Their lives were changed, and I realized that the magic of walking pilgrimages isn't limited to the plains of Spain. Every year for the past ten years, I've led a five-day walking pilgrimage to the Shrine of Our Lady of Good Help in Champion, Wisconsin. I never cease to come away with some new gift, blessing, or lesson learned on the way.

Walking pilgrimages are a much different experience from a bus pilgrimage. When you ride a bus to a shrine, it's mostly about the destination. Pilgrims look forward to a big "Aha" moment waiting for them when they arrive. Walking pilgrims, on the other hand, learn the joy of the journey. Familiar roads look differently when you travel them on foot. Pilgrims begin to appreciate the beauty around them. They enter into the ebb and flow of nature. They draw closer to the people they walk with. They learn to keep their eyes open for encounters with God along the way. Most of all, they learn to put one foot in front of the other and keep walking on good days and bad days. A walking pilgrimage is about more than the destination; it's a journey of the heart. It changes you in ways you never expected.

THE ADVENT JOURNEY

So, what does this have to do with Advent and Christmas? We all struggle with Advent. The Church is telling us to slow down, but the world is telling us, "Hurry up." We rush around preparing for the birth of Jesus. We look forward to the big "Aha" moment waiting for us at Christmas. And we always seem to miss out somehow. How is it that every year Christmas seems less merry and bright than we were hoping it would be? Too often, Christmas seems to fly by even more quickly than Advent does!

The problem is that we keep treating Advent like the bus on the way to Christmas. We expect to step off at Bethlehem and have some experience of Christmas spirit, some kind of "Aha" moment. The fact is that Holy Mother Church designed Advent to be more like a walking pilgrimage. You take a little step every day. You learn to enjoy the journey instead of rushing to Christmas — and then you're better prepared to enjoy the full Christmas season, rather than rushing through one day on your way to the new year. You connect with the people around you. You enter into a new rhythm. The ordinary things of life start to take on a new meaning. God meets you on the road. Think of this book as a Camino guidebook. It will show you how to step off the busy Christmas bus and walk the Advent road one day at a time. You will learn that Advent and Christmas are more than destinations; they involve a journey of the heart.

KEEP WALKING

This book lasts nearly ten weeks, from the First Sunday of Advent on November 30 to the feast of the Presentation on February 2. The feast of the Presentation (also called Candlemas) is the traditional final day after which Christmas decorations must be taken down. Using this book, you will get twenty-eight days to prepare for Christmas and forty days to celebrate Christmas (kind of like the forty days of Lent followed by the fifty days of Easter). We need those extra days. None of the people who saw the Christ Child in person understood the true meaning of Christmas. It was only in the days and years afterward that the "dawn from on high" began to rise in their hearts (see Lk 1:78). The same is true for us in our ongoing journey of faith. Praying with this devotional until February 2 will help you continue to see Jesus in the ordinary. Besides, it's easier to pray in the post-Christmas lull, and we need a little help getting through the low time in January.

You don't have to walk the whole way with me; it's your journey, and you can quit any time. But let me encourage you to plan for a longer walk.

Consider putting up your Christmas tree a little later this year. Put on the lights and ornaments, but don't plug in the lights until the Light of the World is born on December 25. Then keep your tree lit all through the twelve days until January 6. Plan to keep at least your Advent wreath and Nativity scene up until February 2. It may seem like a long way to go now, but you'll be surprised at how quickly it passes. And you'll really enjoy those extra days.

IF YOU MISS A DAY

Even when you are too busy to pray, try to at least open this book and read the Scripture passage each day. If you end up missing a day or two (or even a week), don't try to go back and do all the meditations you missed. Just skip ahead to the current day and pray that one well. It is not important that you do every single meditation. What matters is that you put your heart into your prayer. Prayer is experiencing how our Father looks at you with love. Holiness is learning to live in his long, loving gaze every moment of your life.

NO ONE WALKS ALONE

You might assume because I wrote this book that I'm great at praying. Far from it! I was trained as a spiritual director through the Institute for Priestly Formation. I have taught countless numbers of people how to pray. I've been on pilgrimages and retreats and even a thirty-day silent retreat. But the truth is, unless I'm actually on a retreat or a pilgrimage, I usually pray badly. Most days I'm too busy, distracted, self-absorbed, or lazy to really pray well. And the problem is compounded during the busy Advent and Christmas season. I wrote this book because I need it too! I will be praying with you and for you this whole season. Please pray for me and for your fellow *Oriens* pilgrims. Consider joining me for a virtual Bible study each week. We will meet over Zoom to share our stories of the journey and encourage one another. Visit https://pilgrimpriest.us/book to learn more and sign up for free. We each make our own journey, and every journey is unique, but no one walks alone. *¡Buen Camino!*

— Fr. Joel Sember
Priest, Pastor, Pilgrim

Suggested Calendar for the Advent and Christmas Season

November 30, First Sunday of Advent: Light the first candle on your Advent wreath.

December 6 (Saturday): Give some treats for Saint Nicholas Day.

December 7, Second Sunday of Advent: Light the second candle on your Advent wreath.

December 8 (Monday): Solemnity of the Immaculate Conception. Put up your crèche (manger scene).

December 13 (Saturday): Do some research on traditions surrounding the feast of Saint Lucy.

December 14, Third Sunday of Advent: Light the third (rose) candle on your Advent wreath.

Before December 25: Put up your Christmas tree. Decorate it, but don't plug the lights in. Wait until the Light of the World is born.

December 21, Fourth Sunday of Advent: Light the fourth candle on your Advent wreath.

December 24/25: After attending Christmas Mass, put the baby Jesus in the crèche and light up your Christmas tree. Change the candles in your Advent wreath to white.

December 28 (Sunday): Feast of the Holy Family

January 1 (Thursday): Octave day of Christmas, Solemnity of Mary, Mother of God. Start the new year with Mary.

January 4 (Sunday): Epiphany Observed

January 6 (Tuesday): Epiphany. Have a family party to bless your home with blessed chalk. Afterward, you can take down the tree (if you want to) and the decorations, but don't take down the Advent wreath or the crèche.

January 11: Baptism of the Lord. Official last day of the liturgical season of Christmas.

January 22 (Thursday): A day of penance in the United States in reparation for violations to the dignity of the human person committed through acts of abortion, and prayer for the full restoration of the legal guarantee to the right to life.

February 2 (Monday): Feast of the Presentation. Have one last Christmas party! Light the candles on your wreath and have a family Candlemas procession to the crèche. Sing Christmas carols. Then put away any remaining Christmas decorations.

Blessing of an Advent Wreath

The use of the Advent Wreath is a traditional practice which has found its place in the Church as well as in the home. The blessing of an Advent Wreath takes place on the First Sunday of Advent or on the evening before the First Sunday of Advent. When the blessing of the Advent Wreath is celebrated in the home, it is appropriate that it be led by the father (if present) or the eldest or senior member of the household.

All make the Sign of the Cross together: + In the name of the Father, and of the Son, and of the Holy Spirit.
Leader: Our help is in the name of the Lord.
Response: Who made heaven and earth.
A reading from the Book of the Prophet Isaiah:

> *The people who walked in darkness*
>   *have seen a great light;*
> *Upon those who lived in a land of gloom*
>   *a light has shone.*
> *You have brought them abundant joy*
>   *and great rejoicing;*
> *They rejoice before you as people rejoice at harvest,*
>   *as they exult when dividing the spoils.*
> *For a child is born to us, a son is given to us;*
>   *upon his shoulder dominion rests.*
> *They name him Wonder-Counselor, God-Hero,*
>   *Father-Forever, Prince of Peace.*
> *His dominion is vast*
>   *and forever peaceful,*
>   *Upon David's throne, and over his kingdom,*
>   *which he confirms and sustains*
> *by judgment and justice,*
>   *both now and forever. (9:1–2, 5–6)*

Leader: The word of the Lord.
Response: Thanks be to God.
Leader: Let us pray.

> Lord our God,
> we praise you for your Son, Jesus Christ:
> he is Emmanuel, the hope of the peoples,
> he is the wisdom that teaches and guides us,
> he is the Savior of every nation.
>
> Lord God,
> let your blessing come upon us
> as we light the candles of this wreath.
> May the wreath and its light
> be a sign of Christ's promise to bring us salvation.
> May he come quickly and not delay.
> Through Christ our Lord.

Response: Amen.

The blessing may conclude with a verse from "O Come, O Come, Emmanuel":

> O come, desire of nations, bind
> in one the hearts of humankind;
> bid ev'ry sad division cease
> and be thyself our Prince of peace.
> Rejoice! Rejoice! Emmanuel
> shall come to thee, O Israel.
>
> — From *Catholic Household Blessings & Prayers*

Week One

Lectio Divina

This first week we will use an ancient prayer form called *lectio divina* (pronounced LEK-si-o di-VEE-na). It has four simple steps, known by their Latin names: *lectio* (reading), *meditatio* (meditation), *oratio* (prayer), and *contemplatio* (contemplation). Don't worry about each Latin word. The prayer form is as simple as this: read, think, talk, listen.

We begin with a prayerful reading of a passage from Scripture. We turn over in our minds what we have read: What was the cultural context? What does this particular word mean? What does this mean to me? We chew on the passage for a while. Perhaps a particular word, phrase, or idea speaks to us. But it won't really be prayer if we just stay in our heads. So, we speak to God in our heart or out loud. A conversation takes two, so for the last part of *lectio*, we adopt an attitude of receiving. We are talking, then we are listening. Many people find the *contemplatio* to be a difficult step; they worry about if they are "doing it right" or "if it's really God" whose voice they hear. Don't try too hard. Just be quiet and receive for a little while. Prayer is not so much about getting something from God as it is just being with God. We are using Scripture as a conversation starter, but conversations with God go deeper than words. I'll walk you through it.

Grace of the Week: Each week has a particular theme or focus. The first week will focus on the creation of the world. The simplest things can be the easiest to forget, and the most profound when they are rediscovered. Pray for the grace to wonder anew at the marvel, mystery, and miracle of God's creation.

November 30 — Sunday
First Sunday of Advent

Happy Advent! Do you feel prepared to begin this journey? If you don't feel prepared, then you've come to the right place! Advent is a season of preparation. Doubtless you've heard the parable "A journey of a thousand miles begins with a single step." By opening this book, you are taking the first step on your pilgrimage journey. As the journey continues, you will begin to see the importance of daily prayer. You may already have a great habit of daily prayer. Or you might be hoping to start a habit of daily prayer as part of *Oriens*. Let me review briefly the two ingredients that have helped me to pray well: place and time.

PLACE FOR PRAYER
Where will you pray? If you don't already have a prayer room or a prayer corner, make one. It can be a whole spare room, or as simple as a prayer chair or one side of a couch. Put distractions, like the remote and the mobile phone, out of reach. Hang some pictures or images or an inspiring Scripture quote. It doesn't have to be elaborate. It should be comfortable, free of distractions, and full of things that help you focus on God. Some people like to light a candle while they are praying (but do not leave candles unattended). Plan a *place* for prayer.

TIME FOR PRAYER
When will you pray? I like to pray right away when I get up in the morning. Some people most enjoy this book in the quiet of the evening. It may not happen exactly as you planned every day, but if you don't plan it, odds are it won't happen at all. We make time for the important things in our life, and prayer is the most important thing. Plan a *time* for prayer.

SAINT ANDREW, APOSTLE
Andrew is most famous for introducing his brother Simon Peter to Jesus (see Jn 1:35–42). Andrew is said to have preached the Gospel in Greece, where he suffered martyrdom at Patras. Bound by ropes to an X-shaped cross, he preached to the crowds for two days until he was overcome by

death. He is the patron of Greece, Scotland, and Russia. The white X on the flag of the United Kingdom (the "Union Jack") comes from Saint Andrew. There is a tradition of beginning a Christmas novena on his feast day.

Lectio: Not unsurprisingly, *lectio divina* (divine reading) begins with a *reading* of the text. The Bible is God's word, once spoken through prophets and written by scribes. It has been passed down, copied again and again, and now rendered into English. Far from a dead letter, it continues to be very much alive through the presence and action of the Holy Spirit.

The Spirit intended these words for the original audience that heard them spoken, and again as written prophecies referring to Jesus Christ, and again as words that you would read in this place and time in your life. These words have power. They have the power to touch hearts, change minds, and reveal mysteries. The Spirit has something to say to you today. Ask the Holy Spirit to help you receive the message that is meant for you. *Come, Holy Spirit, enlighten the eyes of my heart (see Eph 1:18).* Then read the passage slowly and prayerfully.

ISAIAH 2:1–5 (LECTIONARY)

This is what Isaiah, son of Amoz, saw concerning Judah and Jerusalem.

In days to come,
the mountain of the Lord's house
shall be established as the highest mountain
and raised above the hills.
All nations shall stream toward it;
many peoples shall come and say:
"Come, let us climb the Lord's mountain,
to the house of the God of Jacob,
that he may instruct us in his ways,
and we may walk in his paths."
For from Zion shall go forth instruction,
and the word of the Lord from Jerusalem.
He shall judge between the nations,

> *and impose terms on many peoples.*
> *They shall beat their swords into plowshares*
> *and their spears into pruning hooks;*
> *one nation shall not raise the sword against another,*
> *nor shall they train for war again.*
> *O house of Jacob, come,*
> *let us walk in the light of the Lord!*

Meditatio: The mountain is a symbol of pilgrimage. As you climb a mountain, the ordinary hustle and bustle of the world fades below you. This is what prayer should do for you. Perhaps picture yourself at the height of a mountain breathing the clean air of the Spirit. What word, phrase, or idea stood out to you as you read the passage? Did something delight you, encourage you, or speak to you in a particular way?

Christmas may seem a long way off. But I would venture to guess that you've had enough Christmases to know what a good one looks and feels like. Perhaps at this stage, you desire the gifts wrapped earlier than ever, your family to all make it home, or perhaps just a little more peace and joy. But let's look just a little bit deeper. Under the surface of Christmas and things going smoothly, what do you more deeply desire? What do you really want for Christmas? Reflect on this question. Then read the passage again, slower this time, and notice the feelings or thoughts that come to you as you read.

Oratio: Now turn to God in prayer. Speak to God the desire(s) of your heart. He's a good listener. This step happens best when your attention shifts from yourself and your reading of Scripture to the God who has been with you this whole time. You might picture yourself on top of the holy mountain, seated in God's house, with the light of God's presence shining upon you. Speak to him from your heart.

Contemplatio: Read the passage a third time. As you read it, keep your attention fixed on God. See all the things that God desires to give his people: light, instruction, peace, unity … What does God desire for you? This time, just receive for a few minutes. Don't try to imagine or invent what God might say. Just ask God, "What is on your heart for me? What is the gift you want to give me for Christmas?" Then be quiet with him and notice whatever emerges in your mind and heart. Spend a few minutes here in a quiet, contemplative mode before you move on. Just be, and be with the Lord, for a little while.

SUGGESTIONS FOR JOURNALING

I often journal as I go, writing notes in the margins or in the journal space below. Throughout your *Oriens* journey, journaling is optional but highly encouraged. The "Suggestions for Journaling" each day are meant to help you pull more out of your meditation. You may not need them; you may have already journaled a small novel at this point. Or you may think nothing happened until you review the questions and realize that you did, in fact, have some kind of experience of God's presence. It's not a test, and these are not review questions. They are just here to help. Use whatever is helpful for you and ignore the rest.

1. The thing I really love about Christmas is …
2. The thing I really hate about Christmas, or found the most challenging about last Christmas, was …
3. I get the most joy from …
4. What do I want to make sure to do? What do I want to make sure not to do this Christmas?
5. I most deeply desire …
6. What is God's desire for my Christmas journey?
7. Where and when will I pray?

November 30 — Sunday

The most important part of our Advent journey is an attitude of thanksgiving. So, finish by saying "Thank You" to God for today's prayer time. Then close with the Saint Andrew Novena Prayer:

> Hail and blessed be the hour and moment in which the Son of God was born of the most pure Virgin Mary, at midnight, in Bethlehem, in the piercing cold. In that hour vouchsafe, I beseech thee, O my God, to hear my prayer and grant my desires, [here mention your request] through the merits of our Savior Jesus Christ, and of His Blessed Mother. Amen.

December 1 — Monday
Monday of the First Week of Advent

Preparation: *Come, Holy Spirit, enlighten the eyes of my heart (see Eph 1:18).*

Lectio: Ask God for the grace to wonder anew at the marvel, mystery, and miracle of creation. We must begin at the beginning, which is exactly the place where the Bible chooses to begin. Thanks to modern science, we have a very different mental picture of the universe. In order to understand parts of this passage, we have to understand how the ancients saw the world. Picture a snow globe. It has a big dome over a heavy, stable base. Inside there are figures that experience snow when you shake the globe. Those figures are like us; we live inside the snow globe. Above our heads is a big blue dome called the *sky*. The stars are like ceiling ornaments stuck inside the dome. The sun and moon travel up one side and down the other. The dome has big floodgates that open to let rain or snow fall on us. Beneath our feet is the underworld, and beneath it all is the abyss, a sort of endlessly deep ocean. Who made the snow globe, and how did we get here? We're glad you asked. Read the Scripture passage through slowly and prayerfully and ask to see this familiar Scripture with fresh eyes. Picture children seated around a campfire listening as a grandfather tells the ancient tale once again.

GENESIS 1:1–8

In the beginning, when God created the heavens and the earth — and the earth was without form or shape, with darkness over the abyss and a mighty wind sweeping over the waters —

Then God said: Let there be light, and there was light. God saw that the light was good. God then separated the light from the darkness. God called the light "day," and the darkness he called "night." Evening came, and morning followed — the first day.

> *Then God said: Let there be a dome in the middle of the waters, to separate one body of water from the other. God made the dome, and it separated the water below the dome from the water above the dome. And so it happened. God called the dome "sky." Evening came, and morning followed — the second day.*

Meditatio: Despite the simplistic cosmology, the biblical author starts in exactly the same place as modern scientists do — with an explosion of light. All of the known matter and energy around us can be traced backward to a single point of expansion, the moment the Bible describes as "Let there be light." God speaks, and his will is done. His word becomes energy and matter, and a whole universe expands into existence and begins cooling into the sky that stretches above us. Scientists say that all the forces in the universe are perfectly balanced to allow our planet to exist. The Bible sees this as a result of careful design. Can you see the design in the universe around you? What must the Creator be like, if his creation is so amazing? Read the passage a second time.

Oratio: What do you think about all this? It might help to reflect on the last time you saw a beautiful sunrise or were far enough from light pollution to catch a glimpse of the star-carpeted night sky. Picture the heavens stretching above us and the vast ocean beneath. Then speak to your Creator. Share with him your wonder at the creation that surrounds you.

Contemplatio: Read the passage one more time. Open your heart to receive whatever God might want to give you. Don't sweat this step. Contemplation is about resting in the mystery, being present to the God who is always present to you and receiving whatever is in his heart for you. Be with the Lord for a few minutes before moving on to the next step.

SUGGESTIONS FOR JOURNALING
1. The part of today's prayer that most delighted me was …
2. I loved the image of …
3. My most noticeable thought or feeling was …
4. I struggled the most with …

5. The rest of the day (or tomorrow, if you pray at night), I plan to try to focus a little bit more on …

Spend a few minutes in wonder and awe at the mystery and marvel of creation that surrounds you! Let gratitude rise in your heart. Then close with an Our Father.

December 2 — Tuesday
Tuesday of the First Week of Advent

Preparation: *Come, Holy Spirit, enlighten the eyes of my heart.* Flip back and briefly review yesterday's prayer time. Start today's prayer with gratitude.

Lectio: Ask God to help you wonder anew at the marvel, mystery, and miracle of his creation. Read the passage below, slowly and prayerfully. God brought something out of nothing. Now he is beginning to organize his creation. Notice what jumps out to you as you read.

GENESIS 1:9–13

> Then God said: Let the water under the sky be gathered into a single basin, so that the dry land may appear. And so it happened: the water under the sky was gathered into its basin, and the dry land appeared. God called the dry land "earth," and the basin of water he called "sea." God saw that it was good. Then God said: Let the earth bring forth vegetation: every kind of plant that bears seed and every kind of fruit tree on earth that bears fruit with its seed in it. And so it happened: the earth brought forth vegetation: every kind of plant that bears seed and every kind of fruit tree that bears fruit with its seed in it. God saw that it was good. Evening came, and morning followed — the third day.

Meditatio: God causes the water to recede until it forms into a giant ocean, covering everything except the pointy bits that are above "sea level." At this point, life begins in the form of all kinds of vegetation. Picture a green planet teeming with an abundance of different forms of plant life. Plants are already complex enough to have a reproductive system and to create seeds, which spread throughout the world. Each plant is brilliantly designed and beautiful in its own way. What do you think as you watch God creating? Why do you think he is doing this? Read the passage again prayerfully.

Oratio: Scientists still do not fully understand photosynthesis. It allows plants to extract energy from the sun and store it in a way that other creatures are able to use. The energy in the coal that powers much of our electricity and in the gasoline that fuels our cars was originally captured from the sun by hard-working plants. Without plants, no complex life forms would be possible. Think of how often we take for granted the contribution plants make to our lives. What else do we take for granted about the world around us? Thank God for all the greenery and speak to him with gratitude.

Contemplatio: Read the passage one more time. The God who made the universe, and is so often taken for granted, enjoys spending time with you. Just open your heart to receive whatever is in God's heart for you — his kindness, mercy, generosity. Spend a few minutes with your maker before moving on.

SUGGESTIONS FOR JOURNALING
1. What are some of the simple but important things that I tend to take for granted?
2. How have I been ungrateful?
3. I am most grateful for …
4. I felt God saying to me …
5. I left prayer wanting …

32 *December 2 — Tuesday*

God is the source of life, but he is often taken for granted. After you've journaled, spend a minute in gratitude for the prayer time you've just had. Then close with an Our Father.

December 3 — Wednesday
Wednesday of the First Week of Advent

ST. FRANCIS XAVIER, MEMORIAL

Francis was the third son born to a noble family in Navarre, now northern Spain, in 1506. As often happened with the younger sons of nobles, he was destined for an ecclesiastical career and sent to the University of Paris. His college roommate was St. Ignatius of Loyola, who was fifteen years older than he and had undergone a profound religious conversion. Francis was won over by Ignatius and became one of the seven founding members of the Society of Jesus (the Jesuits). He was sent to preach the Gospel in the Orient. For ten years he labored tirelessly, bringing more than thirty thousand souls to the light of Christ. His travels took him to India and Japan, and he died on the doorstep of China. How might God be calling you to something greater than your family's plans for you?

Preparation: *Come, Holy Spirit, enlighten the eyes of my heart.* Flip back to yesterday's prayer and recall a blessing you experienced. Spend a minute picturing the expanse of the sky above and the teeming green-and-blue earth beneath. Let gratitude rise in your heart.

Lectio: In your own words, ask God to help you wonder anew at the marvel, mystery, and miracle of his creation. Read today's passage slowly and prayerfully. As you do, picture in your mind the myriad creatures that surround us: giant whales and clever squids, soaring birds and flying insects, bears in their dens and birds in the trees.

GENESIS 1:20-25

> *Then God said: Let the water teem with an abundance of living creatures, and on the earth let birds fly beneath the dome of the sky. God created the great sea monsters and all kinds of crawling living creatures with which the water teems, and all kinds of winged birds. God saw that it was*

good, and God blessed them, saying: Be fertile, multiply, and fill the water of the seas; and let the birds multiply on the earth. Evening came, and morning followed — the fifth day.

Then God said: Let the earth bring forth every kind of living creature: tame animals, crawling things, and every kind of wild animal. And so it happened: God made every kind of wild animal, every kind of tame animal, and every kind of thing that crawls on the ground. God saw that it was good.

Meditatio: Think of the incredible variety of animals that fill the world. There are birds that swim and fish that fly, and insects of every shape and size. Each creature is uniquely adapted to its own ecosystem. All the different species rely on one another in a delicate balance of predator, prey, and prey's prey. And it all starts with plants. What is your favorite kind of animal? What do you find creepy? Each one has its purpose and its place. Read the passage again slowly.

Oratio: We are surrounded with an abundance we can't even fathom. Scientists think that over 80 percent of the world's species, and 90 percent of the world's ocean creatures, have yet to be discovered and classified. And yet, species are going extinct at an alarming rate. We might ever know only a tiny fraction of God's creation. How does this make you feel? What does it tell you about God? What part of creation do you most enjoy, and what part do you find uncomfortable or pointless? Thank God for his creation and share your thoughts with the Creator.

Contemplatio: You have spoken; now take time to listen. Read the passage one more time. This time, receive what God wants to say to you and how God wants to respond to you. Perhaps you receive nothing more than a feeling of peace or presence. Whatever it is, spend a few minutes in silence before you move on.

SUGGESTIONS FOR JOURNALING

1. When it comes to the animals around me, I most enjoy …

2. I am humbled by the realization that …
3. I have a hard time fathoming …
4. I would like someone to explain to me …
5. I ended prayer wanting …

December 4 — Thursday
Thursday of the First Week of Advent

Preparation: *Come, Holy Spirit, enlighten the eyes of my heart.* How has God's love been manifested to you in your prayer time so far? Spend a minute savoring God's loving care for all his creatures and especially his care for you. Let gratitude rise in your heart.

Lectio: In your own words, ask God to help you wonder anew at the marvel, mystery, and miracle of creation. After filling the earth with all kinds of various creatures, God still has one more creature to make: You. Read the passage slowly and prayerfully.

GENESIS 1:26–31

Then God said: Let us make human beings in our image, after our likeness. Let them have dominion over the fish of the sea, the birds of the air, the tame animals, all the wild animals, and all the creatures that crawl on the earth.

> *God created mankind in his image;*
> *in the image of God he created them;*
> *male and female he created them.*

God blessed them and God said to them: Be fertile and multiply; fill the earth and subdue it. Have dominion over the fish of the sea, the birds of the air, and all the living things that crawl on the earth. God also said: See, I give you every seed-bearing plant on all the earth and every tree that has seed-bearing fruit on it to be your food; and to all the wild animals, all the birds of the air, and all the living creatures that crawl on the earth, I give all the green plants for food. And so it happened. God looked at everything he had made, and found it very good. Evening came, and morning followed — the sixth day.

Meditatio: God steps back, as it were, and pauses to think. This final creature will be like all the rest of the animals in important ways, including the fact that it exists as male and female. But it will have two special characteristics: It will be made in the image and likeness of God, and it will exercise dominion over the rest of the animals. In what ways are human beings like God? Why would God choose to create a creature like himself? Read the passage a second time.

Oratio: What does it feel like to have dominion over all the other creatures? Every human being is utterly unique. We each have a unique combination of facial features, physical characteristics, personality, and mental abilities. Your unique combination of genetic code and gene expression (phenotype) never existed before you were conceived, and it will never exist again in the world. You are like all the other creatures and all the other humans, but you are also utterly unique. You are the only *you* that God has ever and will ever make. What thoughts, feelings, or desires are rising in your heart? Turn to the God who made you. Share with him what is on your heart. Be completely honest with him.

Contemplatio: Let God look at you. Creation was not complete without you. God sees you as "very good." Read the passage a third time. Receive what God wants to share with you, what is in his heart for you. Rest in his love for you for a few minutes before moving on.

SUGGESTIONS FOR JOURNALING
1. I exercise dominion over God's creatures when …
2. What is special about me?
3. I saw the image and likeness of God shining in another human being when …
4. I have a hard time accepting that …
5. I sensed God wanting me to know …
6. My deepest desire right now is for …

38 *December 4 — Thursday*

After you've journaled, close with a conversation with God giving thanks for creating you and for listening to you in prayer today. Then pray an Our Father.

December 5 — Friday
Friday of the First Week of Advent

Preparation: *Come, Holy Spirit, enlighten the eyes of my heart.* Think back on yesterday's prayer time (or the last time you prayed if you missed yesterday). How was the experience a blessing for you? Spend a minute being grateful for God's presence and for the things you are learning and the ways you are growing.

Lectio: In your own words, ask God to help you wonder anew at the marvel, mystery, and miracle of his creation. The creation around us comes from God, and it points to God. The marvels of creation are signs of God's wisdom, genius, and care. Can you look beyond creation and catch sight of its Creator? Read the passage slowly and prayerfully. Notice whatever word, phrase, or idea jumps out at you.

PSALM 145

> I will extol you, my God and king;
>   I will bless your name forever and ever.
> Every day I will bless you;
>   I will praise your name forever and ever.
> Great is the Lord and worthy of much praise,
>   whose grandeur is beyond understanding.
> One generation praises your deeds to the next
>   and proclaims your mighty works.
> They speak of the splendor of your majestic glory,
>   tell of your wonderful deeds.
> They speak of the power of your awesome acts
>   and recount your great deeds.
> They celebrate your abounding goodness
>   and joyfully sing of your justice.
> The Lord is gracious and merciful,
>   slow to anger and abounding in mercy.

The Lord is good to all,
   compassionate toward all your works.
All your works give you thanks, Lord
   and your faithful bless you.
They speak of the glory of your reign
   and tell of your mighty works,
Making known to the sons of men your mighty acts,
   the majestic glory of your rule.
Your reign is a reign for all ages,
   your dominion for all generations.
The Lord is trustworthy in all his words,
   and loving in all his works.
The Lord supports all who are falling
   and raises up all who are bowed down.
The eyes of all look hopefully to you;
   you give them their food in due season.
You open wide your hand
   and satisfy the desire of every living thing.
The Lord is just in all his ways,
   merciful in all his works.
The Lord is near to all who call upon him,
   to all who call upon him in truth.
He fulfills the desire of those who fear him;
   he hears their cry and saves them.
The Lord watches over all who love him,
   but all the wicked he destroys.
My mouth will speak the praises of the Lord;
   all flesh will bless his holy name forever and ever.

Meditatio: The proper response of a creature is to praise God. Saint Augustine tells us that the plants, birds, fish, sun, moon, and stars all praise God simply by being what they were made to be and doing what they were made to do. What were we made to be? What was I made to do? Human beings alone can choose to worship God or choose to ignore his presence. We can never stop being the image of God, but our choices make us more like God or more distant from God. Read the passage again slowly, or focus on the word, phrase, or idea that jumped out at you from the first reading.

***Oratio*:** Have you experienced that the Lord is gracious and merciful? Have you had prayers answered? Previous generations, your parents and grandparents, aunts and uncles, spoke the praises of God. Now it is your turn. Speak up, join your voices to the voices of your ancestors and to the voices of all the creatures, and praise God from your heart. If there is something that is blocking you from praising God, some obstacle, doubt, or hurt, then talk to God about it.

***Contemplatio*:** Your praise resounds and echoes into the distance. What does God want to say to you, or give you, in response to the praise you have given him? Maybe it is a thought, word, or feeling. Read the passage a third time, then spend a few minutes letting God look at you with love and gazing back at him. Enjoy the presence of God before you move on.

SUGGESTIONS FOR JOURNALING

1. God is worthy of much praise. Do I make the praise of God part of my daily routine?
2. I am most grateful for …
3. How did the previous generation, my parents and grandparents, aunts and uncles, speak the praises of God?
4. How has the Lord been near to me when I called upon him?
5. I experienced the mercy of God when …
6. I most deeply desire …

42 *December 5 — Friday*

After you've journaled, close with a conversation with God giving thanks for your prayer experience. You may be tempted to skip this step, as you have already been praising and thanking God. It is very important to both begin and end prayer with a spirit of gratitude. Think of it like having coffee with a friend. When you meet up with your friend, you greet them warmly with a hug, a handshake, or kind words. At the end of a conversation, you thank your friend for spending time with you. You wouldn't just get up and walk away. So, spend a minute in thanksgiving before you say goodbye for now. Then pray an Our Father.

December 6 — Saturday
Saturday of the First Week of Advent

SAINT NICHOLAS, BISHOP

Saint Nicholas was the bishop of Myra in modern-day Turkey. He died on this day around AD 350. Very little is known of him apart from the legends that were passed down. It is said that a poor man had three daughters. He had no money to furnish dowries for them and therefore they had no possibility of honorable marriages. Nicholas went secretly at night and threw a bag of gold into the home, then another. The father caught him with the third bag and was finally able to identify his benefactor. There is a tradition of children leaving their shoes out on the eve of his feast and finding them miraculously full of treats, most notably oranges. Practice a little extra generosity today.

REVIEW

Preparation: *Come, Holy Spirit, enlighten the eyes of my heart.* Instead of spending time with a new passage, we will pray with the passages that most spoke to you in this past week. Saint Ignatius called this kind of prayer time a *repetition*. The idea behind a repetition is not so much to do a prayer passage all over again, but to go back to the place you most noticed God's presence and felt loved by God. You return to that place in order to deepen the encounter and the conversation with God. Flip back through your past week's journal entries. Notice what emerged in the conversations. Here are some questions to help you:

1. The prayer time that I enjoyed most and got the most out of was …
2. The prayer time I really struggled with was … What made it hard for me?
3. Where did I notice the presence of God? What did his presence feel like, or how did it affect me?
4. What was God doing, saying, or giving me this week?

5. How did I respond to what God was doing?
6. I'm most grateful for …
7. Is there an image or experience of God's loving presence that emerged from my prayer during this first week? Or was there a word, phrase, or message that really touched me?

Savor that image of God's loving presence. Rest there for a few minutes. Then thank God for today's prayer time and end with an Our Father.

Week Two

Imaginative Prayer

How did *lectio divina* go? If you found yourself struggling, here are a couple of thoughts.

First, don't try too hard. We often think we have to "do prayer right" in order to get something from God. When we put the burden on ourselves, we really aren't open to receive. And receiving isn't hard work. The work comes when we have to let go of our expectations that prayer will happen only if we figure out how to "pray well." In reality, prayer is just noticing and focusing on the presence and action of God in your life. God is present and active all the time. He doesn't talk only during one little part of prayer, and he doesn't stop talking just because you ended your prayer time. Many people find that they receive an answer to their prayer during Mass or before bedtime or at some other moment during the day. The secret is to have an attitude of willingness to receive from God whenever he might be communicating with us.

Secondly, remember that the goal is not to have nice notes in your journal. The goal is quality time with the God who loves you. If you've spent any quality time with God this past week, you've done well. Be careful not to judge your prayer too much. Just be grateful for the first week.

And if you didn't pray at all last week, that's OK. Life gets away from us sometimes. Just pick up with today's prayer and start here.

This week we will learn a new prayer form called imaginative prayer. St. Ignatius of Loyola was the pioneer of this prayer form. He stumbled onto it quite by accident. It changed his life, and he went on to use it to help change other people's lives. Some people are skeptical of this prayer form. They fear it is just creating fantasy air castles. You certainly could do that, but that wouldn't be prayer time. Prayer is about connecting with the God who loves you and is present with you right now. Most of us are only vaguely aware of God's presence. We are much more aware of our current location in space and time, what happened yesterday, and what is on our calendar for today. These are passing things that we need to temporarily unplug from if we want to connect more deeply with God.

A good book or movie will take you out of the present moment for a while and move you to another place and time. In doing so, it can help you connect with something deeper: your own hopes and dreams, your fears, your potential, and what it means to be part of the human condition. In a similar way, imaginative prayer helps connect you with the deeper reality of God's loving presence that is silently behind and beyond all space and time. The imagination is only a conversation starter. Again, if you spend quality time with God, you have achieved your goal.

Grace of the Week: We are surrounded by God's creation. But we are also creatures, created by God the Father and made for a relationship with him. However, we have fallen out of relationship with him. The human race is so used to being separated from God that we have nearly forgotten that we were made by God and for God. Ask God in your own words to help you feel how much our separation from God causes him to suffer so as to desire more strongly a deeper relationship with him.

December 7 — Sunday
Second Sunday of Advent

Preparation: *Come, Holy Spirit, enlighten the eyes of my heart.* Start your prayer with gratitude. Turn back to yesterday and look at the image of God's loving care for you that emerged in your review time. Use your imagination to picture that moment again. Spend about a minute just resting in that experience and savoring the unconditional love with which God loves you.

Set the Scene: Ask God in your own words for the grace to feel the pain of separation from God so as to desire more strongly a deeper relationship with him. Read the passage below. As you do, set the scene in your mind. Picture the Jordan River winding its way through the desert. Picture the large crowds gathering to listen to this roughly clothed man preach repentance and then get dunked in waters of repentance. Picture the fine clothing of the Pharisees and Sadducees who are also coming for a show of righteousness but getting less than a warm welcome.

MATTHEW 3:1-12 (LECTIONARY)

John the Baptist appeared, preaching in the desert of Judea and saying, "Repent, for the kingdom of heaven is at hand!" It was of him that the prophet Isaiah had spoken when he said:

> *A voice of one crying out in the desert,*
> *Prepare the way of the Lord,*
> *make straight his paths.*

John wore clothing made of camel's hair and had a leather belt around his waist. His food was locusts and wild honey. At that time Jerusalem, all Judea, and the whole region around the Jordan were going out to him

*and were being baptized by him in the Jordan River
as they acknowledged their sins.*

*When he saw many of the Pharisees and Sadducees
coming to his baptism, he said to them, "You brood of vipers!
Who warned you to flee from the coming wrath?
Produce good fruit as evidence of your repentance.
And do not presume to say to yourselves,
'We have Abraham as our father.'
For I tell you,
God can raise up children to Abraham from these stones.
Even now the ax lies at the root of the trees.
Therefore every tree that does not bear good fruit
will be cut down and thrown into the fire.
I am baptizing you with water, for repentance,
but the one who is coming after me is mightier than I.
I am not worthy to carry his sandals.
He will baptize you with the Holy Spirit and fire.
His winnowing fan is in his hand.
He will clear his threshing floor
and gather his wheat into his barn,
but the chaff he will burn with unquenchable fire."*

Action! See the face of John the Baptist as he preaches in the spirit and power of Elijah. Picture the faces of the people in the crowd as they acknowledge their sins. Picture the faces of the Pharisees and Sadducees as John singles them out and takes them to task. They aren't used to this kind of treatment. Feel the tension in the air. Who will back down first?

Acknowledge: As you process this scene, notice what is happening in you. What part of the passage do you find most intriguing? What thoughts or feelings are going on inside of you as you picture this passage? Where do you find yourself in the scene? Read the passage a second time.

Relate: Turn to God and share with him what is on your heart. This can be a more challenging part of the prayer. Think of it this way: You are watching John the Baptist preaching repentance. You notice someone is standing next to you on the shores of the Jordan River. You look over and recognize the face of Jesus. He has been watching too. Talk to him about what you see, feel, and think.

Receive: Now turn to Jesus, look at him, and let him look at you. How does he respond to what you have shared? What is in his heart for you? What does he want to say to you or want you to notice? How is he being moved by the face of each person that you imagined earlier? Read the passage a third time, or perhaps just the part that you feel most drawn to. As you do, focus on God and let him speak to you, or just quietly receive what he wants to give you.

Respond: This part is about continuing the conversation. You have shared, you have received something from God, and now you respond to what he gave you. Perhaps you received a sense of peace, and you should say, "Thank you." Or maybe you sensed his care for each person and also for you, and you are moved to realize how much Our Lord cares. Now just receive his care. I'm offering a couple of thoughts only to show you that it's a simple process, like chatting with a friend. Just be with the Lord and savor his loving presence for a minute or two before moving on.

SUGGESTIONS FOR JOURNALING
1. While imagining the scene, what stood out to me was …
2. My strongest thought or feeling during the meditation was …
3. I sensed God communicating to me …
4. I had a sense of joy when …
5. I ended my prayer with a deeper desire for …

54 *December 7 — Sunday*

After you've journaled, end with prayer. Spend a minute thanking God for your prayer experience. Then pray an Our Father.

December 8 — Monday
Solemnity of the Immaculate Conception

The Church has long believed that the Blessed Virgin Mary was preserved free from all sin starting at the very moment of her conception. Christians have celebrated this feast for over 1,200 years, but it was officially declared a dogma by Bl. Pope Pius IX in 1854. Four years later, Our Lady appeared to Saint Bernadette at Lourdes, France, and told her, "I am the Immaculate Conception." Today's feast is a holy day of obligation for Catholics, and the *Gloria* is sung at Mass.

Preparation: *Come, Holy Spirit, enlighten the eyes of my heart.* Call to mind God's loving care for you and spend about a minute just resting in that experience and savoring the unconditional love God has for you. Let gratitude rise in your heart.

Set the Scene: Ask God in your own words for the grace to know how deeply our separation from God pains him so as to desire more strongly a deeper relationship with him. Ephesus is a city in Asia Minor where Saint Paul had labored for two years to preach the Gospel (see Acts 19:10). His letter to them emphasizes the unity of the Church in Christ, who has united both Jews and Gentiles into one body. Picture Saint Paul writing this introduction to his letter. He is reflecting on how God called him from Judaism to Christianity, and how God then called his hearers from their pagan ways to join him in the new Christian religion. He reflects on the people from Ephesus that he has come to know and love. His words are full of gratitude.

EPHESIANS 1:3-6, 11-12 (LECTIONARY)
Brothers and sisters:
Blessed be the God and Father of our Lord Jesus Christ,
who has blessed us in Christ
with every spiritual blessing in the heavens,

as he chose us in him, before the foundation of the world,
to be holy and without blemish before him.
In love he destined us for adoption to himself through Jesus Christ,
in accord with the favor of his will,
for the praise of the glory of his grace
that he granted us in the beloved.

In him we were also chosen,
destined in accord with the purpose of the One
who accomplishes all things according to the intention of his will,
so that we might exist for the praise of his glory,
we who first hoped in Christ.

Action! Do you realize that you, too, were chosen "before the foundation of the world"? Have you felt yourself adopted as a child of God? When have you hoped in Christ?

Acknowledge: How does it feel to be destined, chosen, and adopted? The Immaculate Conception, which we celebrate today, was given to Mary precisely so that Jesus could be born for you and save you from your sins. He made Mary immaculate so that you, too, could be made immaculate. God put even more work into rescuing you than he did into rescuing Noah and creation from the Flood! Sort through what is going on inside of you. Read the passage again and notice your strongest thought, feeling, or desire. Is there a word or phrase that stands out to you?

Relate: God, your secret benefactor, has been unfolding your salvation since before the Big Bang. He is here with you right now. What do you want to say to him? Speak to him in your heart. Share with him what this passage stirred up within you. Just be honest.

Receive: When you are finished sorting and sharing your feelings, read the passage a third time. What does God want to say to you? What is in his heart for you? Don't sweat this step. Many times, God gives something simple like a feeling of peace, a sense of his presence, or a sense that he understands what we are going through.

Respond: Continue the conversation for a few minutes, then just be present to the Lord, and let him be present to you for a few minutes before moving on.

SUGGESTIONS FOR JOURNALING
1. The word, phrase, or idea from this passage that most spoke to me was …
2. I was surprised to realize that …
3. My strongest thought, feeling, or desire was …
4. I saw with new eyes …
5. I ended prayer with a deeper sense that …

58 *December 8 — Monday*

After you've journaled, close with a brief conversation giving thanks to God for your prayer experience. Then close with a Hail Mary.

December 9 — Tuesday
Tuesday of the Second Week of Advent

ST. JUAN DIEGO
On this day in 1532, a native man of what is now Mexico was on his way to daily Mass when he heard a voice calling his name. A beautiful woman was standing on the hill of Tepeyac near present-day Mexico City. She told him that she was the ever-virgin mother of the true God. She wanted him to go speak to the bishop and ask that a church be built on that place so she could manifest her love for all people. The bishop was skeptical and told Juan Diego to come back with a sign. However, that night his uncle took sick. For two days he nursed him, until it seemed that the end was near. He ran to get a priest for the anointing of the sick. Not wanting to run into the lady, he took a route around the other side of the hill, but then he saw her coming down the hill to meet him. She told him not to worry about his uncle, then sent him up the hill to pick some roses, which miraculously were blooming in the December cold. She arranged them with her own hands in his *tilma* (a kind of poncho made of cactus fiber) and then told him to go and show the sign to no one but the bishop himself.

Preparation: *Come, Holy Spirit, enlighten the eyes of my heart.* Call to mind your recent experience of God's loving care. Spend about a minute just resting in that experience and savoring the unconditional love of the Father for his child. Let gratitude rise in your heart.

Set the Scene: Ask God in your own words for the grace to experience how much pain our separation causes God so as to desire more strongly a deeper relationship with him. We have plenty for our imagination. There's a boat full of animals, a giant flood, and Noah is six hundred years old! All the biblical accounts through Genesis 11 are a kind of prehistory of the world, after which human lifespans get more realistic. We shouldn't read this as a literal blow-by-blow historic account of exactly how it happened. Most human civilizations have passed on a Great Flood story. Even Native Americans have a version involving a brave hero who saved the animals in a canoe. We want to tap into the sense that human wickedness has destabilized the world to the point that all life is now under threat. God, however, has set a plan in motion to rescue his creation, and he is working through the one man on earth who will listen to him. Read the passage and set the scene in your mind.

GENESIS 6:12–22

When God saw how corrupt the earth had become, since all mortals had corrupted their ways on earth, God said to Noah: I see that the end of all mortals has come, for the earth is full of lawlessness because of them. So I am going to destroy them with the earth.

Make yourself an ark of gopherwood, equip the ark with various compartments, and cover it inside and out with pitch. This is how you shall build it: the length of the ark will be three hundred cubits, its width fifty cubits, and its height thirty cubits. Make an opening for daylight and finish the ark a cubit above it. Put the ark's entrance on its side; you will make it with bottom, second and third decks. I, on my part, am about to bring the flood waters on the earth, to destroy all creatures under the sky in which there is the breath of life; everything on earth shall perish. I will establish my covenant with you. You shall go into the ark, you and your sons, your wife and your sons' wives with you. Of all living creatures you shall bring two of every kind into the ark, one male and one female, to keep them alive along with you. Of every kind of bird, of every kind of animal, and of every kind of thing that crawls on the ground, two of each will come to you, that you may keep them alive. Moreover, you are to provide yourself with all the food that is to be eaten, and store it away, that it may serve as provisions for you and for them. Noah complied; he did just as God had commanded him.

Action! No one will listen to God except Noah; he alone knows that disaster is coming upon the face of the earth. What would that feel like? Imagine what Noah was thinking and feeling as he went about completing the task God had given him.

Acknowledge: "Noah found favor with the Lord;" he was righteous and blameless in his generation (see Gn 6:8, 9b). Are you open to receive what God wants to give you? God desires to rescue you. Are you listening and responding to God's call? What are you thinking and feeling as you picture the scene? Read the passage a second time.

Relate: Do you fear what God might ask you to do? Are you asking, but not receiving anything from God? Turn to God and share with him what is on your heart. Speak to God honestly whatever you might be thinking or feeling.

Receive: How does God respond to you? Receive whatever it is that God wants to give you — a thought, a word, a feeling, or just a sense of peace or presence. Don't try too hard. Read the passage a third time.

Respond: Whatever you have received from God, respond to it. If you received nothing, be patient. Tell God you will wait, or tell him about your frustration. Know that God loves you and he is with you even if you're not feeling it at this very moment. Just be with God for a minute or two before moving on.

SUGGESTIONS FOR JOURNALING
1. While picturing the scene, I was most struck by …
2. The thing I noticed about Noah was …
3. My strongest thought, feeling, or desire was …
4. The presence of God with me seemed to say to me …
5. I ended prayer with a sense that …

62 *December 9 — Tuesday*

After you've journaled, close with a brief conversation giving thanks to God for your prayer experience. Then pray an Our Father.

December 10 — Wednesday
Wednesday of the Second Week of Advent

Preparation: *Come, Holy Spirit, enlighten the eyes of my heart.* Call to mind a recent experience of God's loving care. Spend about a minute just resting in that experience and savoring the unconditional love with which God loves you. Let gratitude rise in your heart.

Set the Scene: Ask God in your own words for the grace to feel the pain of separation from God so as to desire more strongly a deeper relationship with him. God has appointed man to be the steward of creation. Man's wickedness is capable of not only hurting himself but also of destroying creation. God is the source and author of all life. The Bible says that God did not make death (see Wis 1:13), but when we refused to follow God, we opened the door to the power of death. Only by listening to God and obeying him can mankind and all creation be saved from destruction. Read the passage slowly and prayerfully.

GENESIS 7:11-14,17-21

In the six hundredth year of Noah's life, in the second month, on the seventeenth day of the month: on that day

*All the fountains of the great abyss burst forth,
and the floodgates of the sky were opened.*

For forty days and forty nights heavy rain poured down on the earth.
On the very same day, Noah and his sons Shem, Ham, and Japheth, and Noah's wife, and the three wives of Noah's sons had entered the ark, together with every kind of wild animal, every kind of tame animal, every kind of crawling thing that crawls on the earth, and every kind of bird. ...

> *The flood continued upon the earth for forty days. As the waters increased, they lifted the ark, so that it rose above the earth. The waters swelled and increased greatly on the earth, but the ark floated on the surface of the waters. Higher and higher on the earth the waters swelled, until all the highest mountains under the heavens were submerged. The waters swelled fifteen cubits higher than the submerged mountains. All creatures that moved on earth perished: birds, tame animals, wild animals, and all that teemed on the earth, as well as all humankind.*

Action! Picture the relentless rain, followed by the unstoppable rising flood waters. Even with all our modern technology, rain and floods continue to be mostly out of our control. Every year you can watch dramatic and scary videos of floods occurring in various places in the world, carrying away everything in their path. There is nothing a hapless world can do to save itself from this climate-induced catastrophe. Noah, however, had been listening to God and long ago began taking the necessary steps. How does Noah feel? How does the rest of humanity feel?

Acknowledge: What do you feel as you watch this scene of primordial destruction unfold? You might feel relief, injustice, foreboding, or even anger. Name your feelings but receive them without judging them. What thoughts go through your mind? Read the passage again.

Relate: Picture God gazing at his world with sorrow. If you really need to clean something, you often soak it in soap and water. God doesn't want to destroy everything, but it all needs a good cleaning. Turn to God and share with him what is in your heart — your thoughts, feelings, and desires. Be honest with God, even if you find yourself angry at God. Share your thoughts honestly.

Receive: We probably notice all the death and destruction, but the Bible is keen to point out that God saved the ones he was able to save. How did God feel as he watched the disaster unfold? What was in his heart for Noah and the people of Noah's day? How does God respond to what you have just shared with him? What is in his heart for you? Perhaps you have a hard time looking at God, or receiving what God wants to say to you. Don't be afraid of God's response, but also don't try too hard. Look at God with the eyes of your heart, and let God look at you. Read the passage a third time, or just the part that spoke to you.

Respond: Whatever it is that God has given you, respond to it. The point here is to keep the conversation going until you've said what you needed to say, and received whatever God wanted to give you. Just be with God for a minute or two before moving on.

SUGGESTIONS FOR JOURNALING

1. We've all heard this story before, but praying with it made me realize that …
2. My strongest thought, feeling, or desire was …
3. I told God that …
4. Through God's eyes, I saw differently that …
5. I received a new insight or understanding …
6. I ended prayer wanting …

66 *December 10 — Wednesday*

After you've journaled, close with a brief conversation giving thanks to God for your prayer experience. Then pray an Our Father.

December 11 — Thursday
Thursday of the Second Week of Advent

Preparation: *Come, Holy Spirit, enlighten the eyes of my heart.* Call to mind a recent experience of God's loving care. Spend about a minute just resting in that experience and savoring the unconditional love with which God loves you. Let gratitude rise in your heart.

Set the Scene: Ask God in your own words for the grace to feel the pain of separation from God so as to desire more strongly a deeper relationship with him. Earth has been washed clean, and humanity and creation are given a fresh start. We see allusions to the original creation story in the words, "Be fertile and multiply and fill the earth" (Gn 1:28). Human beings are allowed to eat animals, whereas prior to this point they were only given plants to eat (see Gn 1:29). It is at this point that animals begin to fear human beings. Human beings are not allowed to kill other human beings, except for capital punishment. Read the passage through and set the scene in your mind.

GENESIS 8:18—9:6

So Noah came out, together with his sons and his wife and his sons' wives; and all the animals, all the birds, and all the crawling creatures that crawl on the earth went out of the ark by families.

Then Noah built an altar to the LORD, and choosing from every clean animal and every clean bird, he offered burnt offerings on the altar. When the LORD smelled the sweet odor, the LORD said to himself: Never again will I curse the ground because of human beings, since the desires of the human heart are evil from youth; nor will I ever again strike down every living being, as I have done.

All the days of the earth,

> *seedtime and harvest,*
> *cold and heat,*
> *Summer and winter,*
> *and day and night*
> *shall not cease.*
>
> *God blessed Noah and his sons and said to them: Be fertile and multiply and fill the earth. Fear and dread of you shall come upon all the animals of the earth and all the birds of the air, upon all the creatures that move about on the ground and all the fishes of the sea; into your power they are delivered. Any living creature that moves about shall be yours to eat; I give them all to you as I did the green plants. Only meat with its lifeblood still in it you shall not eat. Indeed for your own lifeblood I will demand an accounting: from every animal I will demand it, and from a human being, each one for the blood of another, I will demand an accounting for human life.*
>
> *Anyone who sheds the blood of a human being,*
> *by a human being shall that one's blood be shed;*
> *For in the image of God*
> *have human beings been made.*

Action! There is a sense of fresh start, of a return to a better spiritual and physical state. The earth is clean again, the animals are saved, and humans can start over. Human beings continue to have evil in their hearts, an evil that could lead to murder and therefore the need for capital punishment. Those who nurture evil and choose to inflict death upon their neighbors will need to be pruned from among us. It's a harsh but necessary means to keep things from spiraling out of control. Read the passage again.

Acknowledge: Notice what stirs up inside of you: thoughts, feelings, desires. God promises not to wipe out the whole human race again with a flood. But that doesn't give us a free pass; he is still concerned about human capacity for evil and still sets limits on human activity. "I'll be watching you" might as well have been the words at the end of this passage. How does that make you feel?

Relate: Turn your heart to God and speak to him. Share with God what this passage stirred up within you. Now let him look at you with love. How does he respond?

Receive: Read the passage a third time. This time receive whatever is in God's heart for you — his thoughts, feelings, desires. How does it make God suffer when he sees his children hurting one another? What does he want for his children? Don't think too hard about this step. Just notice what comes up in the prayer.

Respond: Receive what God has to give you. Then respond in some way. Perhaps you need to say, "I'm sorry." Perhaps God is inviting you to some kind of action. Be with the Lord for a minute or two before moving on.

SUGGESTIONS FOR JOURNALING
1. A new insight or understanding I received was …
2. I felt convicted that …
3. I sensed God communicating to me …
4. I see sin in a new and different light …
5. I ended prayer wanting …

70 *December 11 — Thursday*

After you've journaled, close with a brief conversation giving thanks to God for your prayer experience. Then pray an Our Father.

December 12 — Friday
Friday of the Second Week of Advent

OUR LADY OF GUADALUPE, FEAST
On December 12, 1532, the native called Juan Diego arrived at the bishop's palace clutching something in his *tilma*. He refused to show it to anyone but the bishop. The bishop's servants made him wait for a long time before finally ushering him into the bishop's room. He unfolded his mantle, and Castilian roses tumbled out onto the floor. Even more surprisingly, a miraculous image of the lady herself was imprinted on his *tilma*. The bishop and his entourage accompanied him to check on his uncle, who turned out to be in perfect health. The uncle reported that he had been restored to perfect health after the lady had also appeared to him and told him to name the image thus, "The Perfect Virgin, Holy Mary of Guadalupe." A shrine was built in which to house the miraculous image, and next to it a little house for Juan Diego. He spent the rest of his life telling his story as millions of native Aztecs and Chichimecas converted to the Catholic Faith. The image hangs today in the shrine of Our Lady of Guadalupe on the outskirts of Mexico City. It testifies to her love for all people, including you.

Preparation: *Come, Holy Spirit, enlighten the eyes of my heart.* Be present to the God who is always present to you. Call to mind his loving care for you and spend the first minute of your prayer just resting in the free, unearned gift of loving and being loved. Let gratitude rise in your heart.

Set the scene: Pray for the grace of humility and littleness so that God can unfold his will in your life with all its power and glory. Today's Scripture passage is taken from the Book of Revelation. It is a dramatic and imaginative vision of the struggle between good and evil. Read the passage once to set the scene in your mind.

REVELATION 11:19A; 12:1–6A, 10AB (LECTIONARY)
God's temple in heaven was opened,
and the ark of his covenant could be seen in the temple.

A great sign appeared in the sky, a woman clothed with the sun,
with the moon under her feet,
and on her head a crown of twelve stars.
She was with child and wailed aloud in pain as she labored to give birth.
Then another sign appeared in the sky;
it was a huge red dragon, with seven heads and ten horns,
and on its heads were seven diadems.
Its tail swept away a third of the stars in the sky
and hurled them down to the earth.
Then the dragon stood before the woman about to give birth,
to devour her child when she gave birth.
She gave birth to a son, a male child,
destined to rule all the nations with an iron rod.
Her child was caught up to God and his throne.
The woman herself fled into the desert
where she had a place prepared by God.

Then I heard a loud voice in heaven say:
"Now have salvation and power come,
and the Kingdom of our God
and the authority of his Anointed."

Action: This passage is taken from today's feast day. The image left on Juan Diego's *tilma* shows a woman standing in front of the sun, with the moon under her feet, and wearing a blue-green cloak covered in stars. The sun and moon represented the most powerful Aztec gods. Our Lady is claiming to be more powerful than they are. Yet, she herself is not a god, as she is shown with head bowed and hands folded, reverently praying to God. She is pregnant with God's child.

Acknowledge: Read the passage again. What do you think and feel as you picture the scene? What is the woman feeling? The woman and her child are not afraid to be humble and little, as God protects them and provides for them. Does the thought of humbleness and littleness make you uncomfortable? Do you have a hard time trusting in God's care and protection?

Relate: Where do you see God in today's Scripture passage? Turn to God and speak to him. Share your thoughts, feelings, and desires, the things that were stirred up by today's prayer time.

Receive: Let God respond to what you have shared. Notice whatever thought, feeling, or desire God wants to communicate to you. Read the passage a third time.

Respond: Receive whatever new way God invites you to see this scene in Revelation, the woman, or your own life. Make room in your heart for God's way of seeing things. Then rest in God's love for you for a few minutes before moving on.

SUGGESTIONS FOR JOURNALING
1. I was surprised by …
2. I have a hard time believing that …
3. When I hear the words *humble* and *little*, I think of …
4. I have a newfound appreciation for …
5. I feel God calling me to a new way of seeing, thinking, or acting …

74 *December 12 — Friday*

After you've journaled, close with a brief conversation giving thanks to God for your prayer experience. Then pray a Hail Mary.

December 13 — Saturday
Saturday of the Second Week of Advent

SAINT LUCY, MARTYR, MEMORIAL

Little is known about this young Christian girl from Syracuse in Sicily. It is said that a disappointed suitor denounced her as a Christian, and she was executed in AD 304. She is one of the seven women mentioned by name in the Roman Canon of the Mass (Eucharistic Prayer I). Her name comes from the Latin word *lux*, meaning "light." Because of this, she is the patroness of eyesight. Her feast day is celebrated with the lighting of candles and special foods, particularly in Scandinavian countries. Pray that God will enlighten your heart so as to make you a light for others.

REVIEW

Preparation: *Come, Holy Spirit, enlighten the eyes of my heart.* Call to mind an image of God's loving care for you that has emerged in your prayer. Spend about a minute just resting in that experience and savoring the unconditional love with which God loves you. Let gratitude rise in your heart.

This past week, we started with John the Baptist, survived the Flood with Noah, saw the Mother of God with Juan Diego, and saw God protect the woman and her child from a huge dragon. Flip back through your past week's journal entries. As you do, notice what emerged in the conversation. Here are some questions to help you:

1. Where did I notice God, and what was he doing or saying?
2. How did I respond to what God was doing?
3. I really struggled with …
4. Prayer really seemed to click when …
5. I'm grateful for …
6. Now at the end of this Second Week of Advent, what new meaning or purpose is emerging from my Advent pilgrimage? Perhaps go back and look at your very first day's prayer

time and see what God seems to be wanting from your Advent pilgrimage.
7. Is there one image of God's loving presence that has most clearly spoken to you or touched your heart in this past week?

Conclude by conversing with God about your week. **Acknowledge** what you have been experiencing. **Relate** it to him. **Receive** what he wants to give you. **Respond** to him. Then savor that image of God's loving presence and rest there for a minute or two. Close with an Our Father.

Week Three

The Secret to a Better Advent

How was imaginative prayer? Some people love it, and some people struggle with it. *Lectio divina* can be used with any Scripture passage, but imaginative prayer works best with passages that contain visuals and action. As we move forward, I'll use one or the other prayer form each day, depending on what I think fits with the passage. You don't have to follow my guidance, though. If you prefer one prayer form, you can use it all the time. But let me encourage you to try to become comfortable with either prayer form. Keep in mind that the goal is not nice notes in your journal or amazing imaginative experiences. These two prayer forms are just conversation starters; it is the conversation itself that is key to a good prayer time. Good prayer is about spending quality time with God. If you have spent quality time with God at all this week, you have done well.

MAKING SPACE FOR GOD
If you're having a hard time with consistent prayer, I want to remind you of the importance of time and place. Do you have a dedicated prayer space, prayer corner, or prayer chair? Even one side of a couch will do, as long as you are intentional about keeping prayer items close by and distractions farther away.

What time have you picked for prayer? Is it realistic? If you plan to get up earlier each day, then you need to be going to bed earlier, and also praying a little before bed. How we end our day strongly impacts how the next day begins. If you plan to pray in the evenings, you might need to set an alarm for yourself and be willing to stop doing other things. Modern people try and do "all the things" so we won't miss out on anything. The result is an overstuffed life where nothing is really done well or enjoyed. A good life happens when we decide to spend our time and energy on the important things and let go of things that are good but less important. You will only be able to make quality time for God if you are also willing to sacrifice or reduce other ways you spend your time. Making space for God requires sacrifice. Sacrifices are always fruitful.

MAKING SPACE FOR CHRISTMAS

One of the first set of spiritual experiences I can recall is childhood memories of Christmas disappointment. I always got the presents I dreamed of and more, but the reality of new gifts was somehow less than the anticipation had been. That started me on a quest for a better Christmas. Our world ends its Christmas celebration on the day of Jesus' birth, whereas Catholics aren't supposed to start celebrating until his birthday. Trying to observe Advent, however, makes one feel cheated out of Christmas. Eventually I discovered the eight days of Christmas (the octave), the twelve days of Christmas (to January 6, the Epiphany), and the forty days of Christmas (ending on February 2, the feast of the Presentation). Celebrating these extra feast days allows us see Christmas as a celebration that begins on December 25 and continues for forty days. When you shift Christmas forward, you also make time for Advent right now. I have come to really enjoy waiting to light the Christmas tree and then savoring it as long as it lasts into January. Don't feel bad if you've already been playing Christmas music since before Thanksgiving. Just try a little Christmas in January this year and see what you think of it.

Grace of the Week: God has a plan to restore creation and undo the effects of sin. We need a Savior, and God has just the thing. We will pray with Scripture passages that give us examples of faith to inspire us and prepare us for the final nine-day countdown to Christmas. Ask God for the grace of humility and littleness so that he can unfold his will in your life with all its power and glory.

December 14 — Sunday
Third Sunday of Advent

Preparation: *Come, Holy Spirit, enlighten the eyes of my heart.* Be present to the God who is always present to you. Call to mind his loving care for you and spend the first minute of your prayer just resting in the free, unearned gift of loving and being loved. Let gratitude rise in your heart.

Set the Scene: Pray for the grace of humility and littleness so that God can unfold his will in your life with all its power and glory. John the Baptist appears again; perhaps flip back to last Sunday's reading (pp. 51–52), or just recall how you imagined the scene. John has not seen any of the works of Jesus with his own eyes. After baptizing the Messiah in Matthew chapter 3, John is subsequently arrested (see Mt 4:12). Picture him holed up in a dank prison in the basement of Herod's castle. Rumors of Jesus' miracles have come to John, and he sends his disciples to ask Jesus the all-important question. Read the passage and set the scene in your mind.

MATTHEW 11:2-11 (LECTIONARY)

> When John the Baptist heard in prison of the works of the
>   Christ,
> he sent his disciples to Jesus with this question,
> "Are you the one who is to come,
> or should we look for another?"
> Jesus said to them in reply,
> "Go and tell John what you hear and see:
> the blind regain their sight,
> the lame walk,
> lepers are cleansed,
> the deaf hear,
> the dead are raised,
> and the poor have the good news proclaimed to them.
> And blessed is the one who takes no offense at me."
>
> As they were going off,

> *Jesus began to speak to the crowds about John,*
> *"What did you go out to the desert to see?*
> *A reed swayed by the wind?*
> *Then what did you go out to see?*
> *Someone dressed in fine clothing?*
> *Those who wear fine clothing are in royal palaces.*
> *Then why did you go out? To see a prophet?*
> *Yes, I tell you, and more than a prophet.*
> *This is the one about whom it is written:*
> *Behold, I am sending my messenger ahead of you;*
> *he will prepare your way before you.*
> *Amen, I say to you,*
> *among those born of women*
> *there has been none greater than John the Baptist;*
> *yet the least in the kingdom of heaven is greater than he."*

Action! Is John having doubts? He predicted a Messiah mightier than himself, saying, "He will clear his threshing floor and gather his wheat into his barn, but the chaff he will burn with unquenchable fire" (Mt 3:12). Jesus has turned out rather meek and mild in comparison. On the other hand, perhaps John's faith is stronger than ever, and he wants to encourage his disciples to transfer their allegiance to Jesus. Picture the crowd gathered around Jesus and listening intently as the disciples arrive with their question.

Acknowledge: Perhaps your Advent pilgrimage is not going as you had hoped. Perhaps you feel behind in your Christmas preparations. Have you found yourself discouraged with a lack of results, or prayer times that were missed or did not go according to plan? When have you felt disappointed with yourself, the events in the world, the Church, or even God himself? Listen to your feelings and acknowledge them. Read the passage again.

Relate: Jesus is listening intently to you. Speak to him what is on your heart — your thoughts, feelings, or desires. How does Jesus receive what you want to say to him? He already knows, and he's been waiting for you to ask. Let him look at you with love.

Receive: What is in Jesus' heart for you? Perhaps he responds with another question, like he does in today's Gospel. Perhaps he invites you to a different way of seeing your situation or reminds you of something you had forgotten. It's your turn to listen and receive. Read the passage a third time.

Respond: The conversation continues, or perhaps you are comfortable just sitting with the Lord. Can you receive his love for you? Do you still have your doubts? Talk and listen, back and forth, for as long as you need to. Now just be with the Lord for a minute or two before moving on.

SUGGESTIONS FOR JOURNALING
1. While imagining the scene, what stood out to me was …
2. I struggle to accept the fact that …
3. I sensed God communicating to me …
4. I feel God calling me to a new way of thinking or acting …
5. I ended prayer with a deeper sense that …

86 *December 14 — Sunday*

After you've journaled, close with a brief conversation giving thanks to God for your prayer experience. Then pray an Our Father.

December 15 — Monday
Monday of the Third Week of Advent

Preparation: *Come, Holy Spirit, enlighten the eyes of my heart.* Call to mind an image of God's loving care for you that has emerged in your prayer. Spend about a minute just resting in that experience and savoring the unconditional love with which God loves you. Let gratitude rise in your heart.

Set the Scene: This is Joshua's final discourse to the people of Israel, after they have defeated the city of Jericho and settled in the promised land. Though the Jewish people have seen God do great things, they are surrounded by pagan nations that worship many gods. Joshua wants to leave them with a final exhortation to listen to the one true God. Read the passage slowly and prayerfully.

JOSHUA 24:1-2A, 3-7AB, 11, 13-15

Joshua gathered together all the tribes of Israel at Shechem, summoning the elders, leaders, judges, and officers of Israel. When they stood in ranks before God, Joshua addressed all the people: "Thus says the Lord, the God of Israel: I brought your father Abraham from the region beyond the River and led him through the entire land of Canaan. I made his descendants numerous, and gave him Isaac. To Isaac I gave Jacob and Esau. To Esau I assigned the mountain region of Seir to possess, while Jacob and his children went down to Egypt.

"Then I sent Moses and Aaron, and struck Egypt with the plagues and wonders that I wrought in her midst. Afterward I led you out. And when I led your ancestors out of Egypt, you came to the sea, and the Egyptians pursued your ancestors to the Red Sea with chariots and charioteers. When they cried out to the Lord, he put darkness

between you and the Egyptians, upon whom he brought the sea so that it covered them. Your eyes saw what I did to Egypt. Once you crossed the Jordan and came to Jericho, the citizens of Jericho fought against you, but I delivered them also into your power. I gave you a land you did not till and cities you did not build, to dwell in; you ate of vineyards and olive groves you did not plant.

"Now, therefore, fear the Lord and serve him completely and sincerely. Cast out the gods your ancestors served beyond the River and in Egypt, and serve the Lord. If it is displeasing to you to serve the Lord, choose today whom you will serve, the gods your ancestors served beyond the River or the gods of the Amorites in whose country you are dwelling. As for me and my household, we will serve the Lord."

Action! As the Israelites stand before Joshua, some may have foreign idols hidden in their tents or amulets under their clothing. These other gods promised fertility, success in war, riches, and many other blessings. It's not such an easy choice to part with them. Imagine the struggle going on in each heart and in each family. How faithful are you to the true God? How faithful do you want to be?

Acknowledge: Juan Diego grew up with the Aztec gods. Fed by human sacrifice, they promised the people victory and prosperity. He had made the brave choice to abandon his ancestral gods to follow the God preached by the Spanish friars. What was that choice like for him? Is God really first in your life, or have you allowed other things to take the first place? Notice your thoughts, feelings, and desires. Read the passage again.

Relate: God is listening as Joshua invites the people to this covenant ritual. He recounts all the wonderful deeds God has done for them. Though they owe God a debt they can never repay, God does not want slaves, but sons. God has done great things for you, but God will let you walk away if you choose not to serve him. He values your freedom. In fact, he created it as a gift for you. How will you use your freedom? Speak to him in your heart. Share with God whom you have decided to serve. If you have questions or fears or difficulties, don't be afraid to share those with God as well.

Receive: Read the passage a third time, or just read the part that speaks to you. Be open to what God wants to say to you, without fear or expectation. Perhaps you will be reminded of a previous commitment, of God's mercy, or he will give you a sense of peace or confidence in his presence. Just notice whatever thought, feeling, or desire comes back to you in response to your honesty.

Respond: Converse with the Lord for a minute or two, and then spend a few minutes savoring his merciful love for you and all the great things he has done for you.

SUGGESTIONS FOR JOURNALING
1. I felt convicted by …
2. The word, phrase, or idea that most spoke to me was …
3. I see the love of God in a new way …
4. I feel that God is calling me to …
5. My biggest obstacle to following God wholeheartedly is …
6. God wanted me to know …
7. I ended prayer with a stronger desire for …

90 *December 15 — Monday*

After you've journaled, close with a brief conversation giving thanks to God for your prayer experience. Then pray an Our Father.

December 16 — Tuesday
Tuesday of the Third Week of Advent

Preparation: *Come, Holy Spirit, enlighten the eyes of my heart.* Call to mind God's loving presence and spend the first minute of your prayer just resting in the free, unearned gift of loving and being loved. Let gratitude rise in your heart.

Lectio: Ask God in your own words for the grace of humility and littleness so that God can unfold his will in your life with all its power and glory. The Letter to the Hebrews wants to show us that faith is the ticket to a life that pleases God. We often think of faith in terms of what we believe. We use phrases like "teaching the Faith" or "He knows the Faith." But the biblical sense of faith is better understood along the lines of faithfulness or trustworthiness. Abel, Enoch, and Noah were faithful to God. They themselves trusted God. They listened to God and did his will, which in turn made them trustworthy. They trusted God, and God could trust them. Read the passage slowly and prayerfully.

HEBREWS 11:1–7

Faith is the realization of what is hoped for and evidence of things not seen. Because of it the ancients were well attested. By faith we understand that the universe was ordered by the word of God, so that what is visible came into being through the invisible. By faith Abel offered to God a sacrifice greater than Cain's. Through this he was attested to be righteous, God bearing witness to his gifts, and through this, though dead, he still speaks. By faith Enoch was taken up so that he should not see death, and "he was found no more because God had taken him." Before he was taken up, he was attested to have pleased God. But without faith it is impossible to please him, for anyone who approaches God must believe that he exists and that he rewards those who seek him. By faith Noah, warned about what was not yet seen, with reverence built an ark for the salvation of his household. Through this he condemned the world and inherited the righteousness that comes through faith.

Meditatio: We have a hard time trusting people when we don't know them very well. Faith springs from a personal relationship. By "personal," I don't mean private (not a "personal" pan pizza), but rather a relationship between persons (like receiving a "personal" message). What is the personal message God wants to send you? How is God inviting you to trust him more deeply?

Oratio: Read the passage a second time. Notice the thoughts, feelings, and desires that are rising within you. Do you find it hard to trust God? Do you doubt that God would want a relationship with you? Do you have some good reasons to doubt that you can trust God? Or have you made promises to put God first only to fall back into the same bad habits again and again? On the other hand, you might find yourself grateful for the gift of faith, asking that it increase, and celebrating people you know who have faith. Read the passage a third time, but this time focus on the work that God did in and through those who trusted him.

Contemplatio: Continue to focus on God. Receive his love for you and whatever he wants to give you. Just be with the Lord for a minute or two and allow your faith to increase before moving on.

SUGGESTIONS FOR JOURNALING

1. I could add to the list of Abel, Enoch, and Noah with people (family, friends, and fellow church members) who I know personally, in particular …
2. I want to trust God, but I feel that he let me down when …
3. I have a hard time believing God would put his trust in me because …
4. My faith in God grew when …
5. The personal message God had for me was …

After you've journaled, close with a brief conversation giving thanks to God for your prayer experience. Then pray an Our Father.

December 17 — Wednesday
Countdown to Christmas: 9

O Wisdom of our God Most High,
guiding creation with power and love:
come to teach us the path of knowledge!

Nine days before Christmas, the Advent season switches gears. The lectionary provides readings from the Gospel passages that immediately precede the birth of Jesus. Each day is assigned a special "O Antiphon," a poetic invocation that draw on Old Testament prophecies, which foretell who the coming Messiah is and what he will do. We will pray with the daily lectionary readings now until Christmas. These Gospel passages from Matthew and Luke will be familiar to you. Perhaps you even prayed with them last year. As you pray with them again, you will begin to see the genius of the liturgical year. We return to the same Scriptures and feasts as last year, but they aren't the same experience, because we have changed. New insights and spiritual experiences build on the previous year's experiences. God is, as Saint Augustine said, "ever ancient, ever new." Let's see what new things God has in store for you this year.

Preparation: *Come, Holy Spirit, enlighten the eyes of my heart.* Be present to the God who is always present to you. Call to mind his loving care for you and spend the first minute of your prayer just resting in the free, unearned gift of loving and being loved. Let gratitude rise in your heart.

Lectio: Ask God for the grace of humility and littleness so that he can unfold his will in your life with all its power and glory. Read the passage slowly and prayerfully. Underline the names you recognize as you go along.

MATTHEW 1:1–17 (LECTIONARY)
The book of the genealogy of Jesus Christ,
the son of David, the son of Abraham.

*Abraham became the father of Isaac,
Isaac the father of Jacob,
Jacob the father of Judah and his brothers.
Judah became the father of Perez and Zerah,
whose mother was Tamar.
Perez became the father of Hezron,
Hezron the father of Ram,
Ram the father of Amminadab.
Amminadab became the father of Nahshon,
Nahshon the father of Salmon,
Salmon the father of Boaz,
whose mother was Rahab.
Boaz became the father of Obed,
whose mother was Ruth.
Obed became the father of Jesse,
Jesse the father of David the king.*

*David became the father of Solomon,
whose mother had been the wife of Uriah.
Solomon became the father of Rehoboam,
Rehoboam the father of Abijah,
Abijah the father of Asaph.
Asaph became the father of Jehoshaphat,
Jehoshaphat the father of Joram,
Joram the father of Uzziah.
Uzziah became the father of Jotham,
Jotham the father of Ahaz,
Ahaz the father of Hezekiah.
Hezekiah became the father of Manasseh,
Manasseh the father of Amos,
Amos the father of Josiah.
Josiah became the father of Jechoniah and his brothers
at the time of the Babylonian exile.*

After the Babylonian exile,

Jechoniah became the father of Shealtiel,
Shealtiel the father of Zerubbabel,
Zerubbabel the father of Abiud.
Abiud became the father of Eliakim,
Eliakim the father of Azor,
Azor the father of Zadok.
Zadok became the father of Achim,
Achim the father of Eliud,
Eliud the father of Eleazar.
Eleazar became the father of Matthan,
Matthan the father of Jacob,
Jacob the father of Joseph, the husband of Mary.
Of her was born Jesus who is called the Christ.

Thus the total number of generations
from Abraham to David
is fourteen generations;
from David to the Babylonian exile, fourteen generations;
from the Babylonian exile to the Christ,
fourteen generations.

Meditatio: We often roll our eyes at the biblical genealogy because of the unpronounceable names. But these were real people who really lived. You may not know all these names, but God knows every single person on this list, and they are all precious to him. The remains of each one are buried somewhere here on earth, and God knows the resting place of them all. Some of them were famous saints and others are rather infamous. The lineage of the Messiah is just as messy as your family history and mine (see Gn 38). Yet, each one is an important link in an unbroken chain of ancestors that would give birth to God's son. If there had been no Abiud, there would have been no Jesus. All along, he was guiding creation with power and love. What does your bloodline look like? How might God be using you, your family, and other apparently ordinary people to play a part in his extraordinary plans? Reflect for a few minutes, then read the passage again slowly. Notice your thoughts and feelings and the part that most speaks to you.

Oratio: Do you question your value? Do you wonder if God really has a plan? Do you sometimes feel insignificant or a burden to others? Share your thoughts, feelings, and desires with the God who created you. Be honest with him.

Contemplatio: Read the passage again, or just the part that spoke to you. Open your heart to receive what God wants to give you. Your life is a precious link in the chain of humanity. Receive whatever God wants to show you or give you: a word, image, or thought. But maybe you also will have a bit of a conversation. God is with you in this ordinary moment. You matter to him. Rest in and savor his love for you.

SUGGESTIONS FOR JOURNALING

1. I see God's hand in my own personal history when …
2. Because of my family or past, I struggle with …
3. I sensed God communicating to me …
4. I see my family history in a new light …
5. Optional: Write out your own genealogy after the style of this Scripture passage. Spend time praying for each of your ancestors.

98 *December 17 — Wednesday*

After you've journaled, close with a brief conversation of thanksgiving to God for today's prayer time. Then pray an Our Father.

December 18 — Thursday
Countdown to Christmas: 8

*O Leader of the House of Israel,
giver of the Law of Moses on Sinai:
come to rescue us with your mighty power!*

Preparation: *Come, Holy Spirit, enlighten the eyes of my heart.* Be present to the God who is always present to you. Call to mind his loving care for you and spend the first minute of your prayer just resting in the free, unearned gift of loving and being loved. Let gratitude rise in your heart.

Set the Scene: Ask God for the grace of humility and littleness so that he can unfold his will in your life with all its power and glory. The betrothal of Mary and Joseph was a legal marriage. In accordance with the traditions of the time, young people married early and then prepared to live together. Joseph would have been preparing a place for his wife at his father's house. Picture the progress of this construction project: Where was Joseph sleeping? Use your imagination to set the scene. Read through this passage slowly and prayerfully.

MATTHEW 1:18–25 (LECTIONARY)
*This is how the birth of Jesus Christ came about.
When his mother Mary was betrothed to Joseph,
but before they lived together,
she was found with child through the Holy Spirit.
Joseph her husband, since he was a righteous man,
yet unwilling to expose her to shame,
decided to divorce her quietly.
Such was his intention when, behold,
the angel of the Lord appeared to him in a dream and
said,
"Joseph, son of David,*

do not be afraid to take Mary your wife into your home.
For it is through the Holy Spirit
that this child has been conceived in her.
She will bear a son and you are to name him Jesus,
because he will save his people from their sins."
All this took place to fulfill
what the Lord had said through the prophet:

> Behold, the virgin shall be with child and bear a son,
> and they shall name him Emmanuel,

which means "God is with us."
When Joseph awoke,
he did as the angel of the Lord had commanded him
and took his wife into his home.
He had no relations with her until she bore a son,
and he named him Jesus.

Action! Adultery was not only a sin, but it was also a crime punishable by stoning to death. "Divorcing her quietly" would mean not denouncing her as an adulteress. It would mean, in essence, that the whole town thought Joseph was a deadbeat dad who had got his wife pregnant and then refused to live with her. It was God who gave the law that put Joseph in this predicament. Yet, God will also show him a way through. God sees Joseph's willingness to sacrifice for his wife and invites him to a different form of sacrifice. What did it mean to Joseph to hear "God is with us" in his difficult situation? What does Joseph experience through this dream? What does he think or feel? How does he act on the new information?

Acknowledge: When have you been called to sacrifice? When has the presence of God helped you through a difficult conundrum? Notice your strongest thought, feeling, or desire. Read the passage a second time.

Relate: Speak to God about what is on your heart. Let him look at you with love. How does he respond?

Receive: Receive whatever is in God's heart for you — his thoughts, feelings, desires. Read the passage a third time.

Respond: Now answer him back again. Just be with the Lord for a minute or two before moving on.

SUGGESTIONS FOR JOURNALING
1. I found God in the midst of my struggles when …
2. My greatest fear or struggle seems to be …
3. I sensed God communicating to me …
4. I feel peace when …
5. God's love is inviting me to a new way of seeing, thinking, or acting today, as Christmas is now just one week away …

102 *December 18 — Thursday*

After you've journaled, close with a brief conversation thanking God for today's prayer time. Then pray an Our Father.

December 19 — Friday
Countdown to Christmas: 7

O Root of Jesse's stem,
sign of God's love for all his people:
come to save us without delay!

Preparation: *Come, Holy Spirit, enlighten the eyes of my heart.* Be present to the God who is always present to you. Call to mind his loving care for you and spend the first minute of your prayer just resting in the free, unearned gift of loving and being loved. Let gratitude rise in your heart.

Set the Scene: Ask God for the grace of humility and littleness so that he can unfold his will in your life with all its power and glory. As you do, set the scene in your mind. We see an old priest going about his daily duties. What does the Temple look like? What does the angel look like? Picture the people outside waiting for Zechariah to emerge from the smoky, incense-filled Temple.

LUKE 1:5–25 (LECTIONARY)

In the days of Herod, King of Judea,
there was a priest named Zechariah
of the priestly division of Abijah;
his wife was from the daughters of Aaron,
and her name was Elizabeth.
Both were righteous in the eyes of God,
observing all the commandments
and ordinances of the Lord blamelessly.
But they had no child, because Elizabeth was barren
and both were advanced in years.

Once when he was serving as priest
in his division's turn before God,

*according to the practice of the priestly service,
he was chosen by lot
to enter the sanctuary of the Lord to burn incense.
Then, when the whole assembly of the people was praying outside
at the hour of the incense offering,
the angel of the Lord appeared to him,
standing at the right of the altar of incense.
Zechariah was troubled by what he saw, and fear came upon him.*

*But the angel said to him, "Do not be afraid, Zechariah,
because your prayer has been heard.
Your wife Elizabeth will bear you a son,
and you shall name him John.
And you will have joy and gladness,
and many will rejoice at his birth,
for he will be great in the sight of the Lord.
He will drink neither wine nor strong drink.
He will be filled with the Holy Spirit even from his mother's womb,
and he will turn many of the children of Israel
to the Lord their God.
He will go before him in the spirit and power of Elijah
to turn the hearts of fathers toward children
and the disobedient to the understanding of the righteous,
to prepare a people fit for the Lord."*

*Then Zechariah said to the angel,
"How shall I know this?
For I am an old man, and my wife is advanced in years."
And the angel said to him in reply,
"I am Gabriel, who stand before God.
I was sent to speak to you and to announce to you this good news.
But now you will be speechless and unable to talk*

until the day these things take place,
because you did not believe my words,
which will be fulfilled at their proper time."
Meanwhile the people were waiting for Zechariah
and were amazed that he stayed so long in the sanctuary.
But when he came out, he was unable to speak to them,
and they realized that he had seen a vision in the sanctuary.
He was gesturing to them but remained mute.

Then, when his days of ministry were completed, he went home.

After this time his wife Elizabeth conceived,
and she went into seclusion for five months, saying,
"So has the Lord done for me at a time when he has seen fit
to take away my disgrace before others."

Action! Today's antiphon is drawn from Isaiah 11:1–10. King David's line had long ago been "cut off" from royal power. But God would be raising up a new shoot from the "stump of Jesse" (King David's father), and "his dwelling shall be glorious." In a similar way, Zechariah and Elizabeth have long given up the dream of having their own child. Even though Zechariah is ministering in the Temple, the last thing he expects is for an angel to emerge from the clouds of incense. What does he think or feel when the angel unexpectedly appears to him? How does he feel when he realizes that God is answering his prayer? How does Elizabeth feel when her husband returns home?

Acknowledge: Even though you are praying, and have connected with God in the past, do you doubt that God is present or will speak to you in a way you can understand? Is there a particular word, phrase, or moment that jumps out at you from this reading? What thoughts or feelings are stirred up by this reading? What is the desire of your heart? Read the passage a second time.

Relate: Speak to God about the desires of your heart. Do you believe he is listening and will answer your prayers? Let him look at you with love. How does he respond?

Receive: Read the passage a third time, or just the part that spoke to you. Open your heart to believe in God's presence with you and to receive whatever is in God's heart for you — his thoughts, feelings, desires, his Good News for you. Do you believe that God can and will do good things in your life?

Respond: Continue the conversation. Enjoy God's loving presence with you in your current place of prayer before moving on.

SUGGESTIONS FOR JOURNALING
1. The thing that spoke to me most was …
2. I felt God stirring up a desire for …
3. I have a hard time trusting when …
4. My greatest fear or struggle seems to be …
5. I sensed God was with me and wanted me to know …

After you've journaled, close with a brief conversation giving thanks to God for being with you in your prayer today. Then pray an Our Father.

December 20 — Saturday
Countdown to Christmas: 6

O Key of David,
opening the gates of God's eternal Kingdom:
come and free the prisoners of darkness!

Preparation: *Come, Holy Spirit, enlighten the eyes of my heart.* Be present to the God who is always present to you. Call to mind his loving care for you and spend the first minute of your prayer just resting in the free, unearned gift of loving and being loved. Let gratitude rise in your heart.

Set the Scene: Ask God for the grace of his loving presence with you, Emmanuel, to break into your daily life and take root in your heart. Read the passage through. Tradition usually sets the Annunciation at Mary's home in Nazareth. What time of day was it? Perhaps Mary has paused from her chores for a little prayer time. Use your imagination to set the scene.

LUKE 1:26–38 (LECTIONARY)

In the sixth month,
the angel Gabriel was sent from God
to a town of Galilee called Nazareth,
to a virgin betrothed to a man named Joseph,
of the house of David,
and the virgin's name was Mary.
And coming to her, he said,
"Hail, full of grace! The Lord is with you."
But she was greatly troubled at what was said
and pondered what sort of greeting this might be.
Then the angel said to her,
"Do not be afraid, Mary,
for you have found favor with God.
Behold, you will conceive in your womb and bear a son,

and you shall name him Jesus.
He will be great and will be called Son of the Most High,
and the Lord God will give him the throne of David his father,
and he will rule over the house of Jacob forever,
and of his Kingdom there will be no end."

But Mary said to the angel,
"How can this be,
since I have no relations with a man?"
And the angel said to her in reply,
"The Holy Spirit will come upon you,
and the power of the Most High will overshadow you.
Therefore the child to be born
will be called holy, the Son of God.
And behold, Elizabeth, your relative,
has also conceived a son in her old age,
and this is the sixth month for her who was called barren;
for nothing will be impossible for God."

Mary said, "Behold, I am the handmaid of the Lord.
May it be done to me according to your word."
Then the angel departed from her.

Action! Play the scene forward in your mind. Today's O Antiphon takes the key of David (see Is 22:22) in two different directions: It will open the kingdom of heaven that was closed by the sin of Adam and Eve, and it will unlock the prisoners who have been kept in darkness by that same sin. But the key doesn't have the power to unlock Mary's womb; only she can do that. All of creation, groaning under the sentence of sin, awaits her answer with bated breath. Why is this virgin greatly troubled at the angel's words? What is in her heart at this moment? What does her yes feel like for her?

Acknowledge: Notice what is going on inside of you. Do you sometimes have a hard time accepting God's plans for your life? Is God waiting for you to "unlock" your heart to him? Read the passage a second time.

Relate: Speak to Mary about your thoughts and feelings. Together with her, turn to God in prayer. Share what is on your heart with complete honesty. Question God, as Mary questioned the angel. Don't hide your feelings from God.

Receive: Receive whatever is in God's heart for you — his thoughts, feelings, desires. He did all this for you. What more does he want to give you? If you have a hard time receiving, ask Mary to show you how to receive. Read the passage a third time, or just the part that speaks to you.

Respond: God wants to dwell in your heart as he dwelt in the womb of Mary. Cherish the gift of God's love, not only for you and with you, but even within you. Converse with God in your heart. Then just be with the Lord and with Mary for a minute or two before moving on.

SUGGESTIONS FOR JOURNALING
1. My heart is troubled by …
2. How have I responded when God's plans interrupted my plans?
3. God's presence feels like …
4. I sensed God was with me and wanted me to know …
5. I ended prayer wanting …

After you've journaled, close with a brief conversation with God giving thanks for your prayer experience. Then pray a Hail Mary.

REVIEW
Let's take a few minutes to look back at the past week.

1. Where did I notice God, and what was he doing or saying?

112 December 20 — Saturday

2. I struggled with ...
3. I'm grateful for ...
4. Were there any concerns, fears, worries or questions I raised early in the week that were answered by my prayer times later in the week?
5. A key theme seems to be ...
6. I was most able to rest in God's love for me when ...
7. What I really desire most for Christmas is ...

Conclude by conversing with God about your review. **Acknowledge** what you have been experiencing. **Relate** it to him. **Receive** what he wants to give you. **Respond** to him. Then savor that image of God's loving presence and rest there for a minute or two. Then read today's Scripture one more time as a prayer of praise and thanksgiving.

Week Four

Making Prayer Happen When You Get Busy

Half an hour's meditation each day is essential, except when you are busy. Then a full hour is needed.
— *St. Francis de Sales*

My Advent often follows the same pattern. The first week or two, I find the season to be surprisingly enjoyable. I remark that I don't feel rushed this year and I look forward, finally, to a peaceful and prayerful Christmas. Then everything hits at once — Christmas cards start to pile up, I have not yet sent cards, I still have gifts to purchase, and now last-minute planning for the Christmas season is upon me. My general habit is to freak out, get angry, and mutter under my breath, "I hate this season. Bah humbug!"

One year, when I became so overwhelmed, I quit trying at all. I just sat in my prayer space and prayed a full, solid holy hour. I may have stayed even longer than an hour; since I wasn't going to catch up, what difference did it make? Then I wandered over to the office and, to my surprise, accomplished far more than I ever thought possible. This is the paradox of prayer. When I focus on the work, instead of God, the work piles up. When I focus on God, instead of the work, the work gets done.

This is why I encourage you not to try and catch up if you miss a day. Or a week. Or are finally opening the book for the first time. *Oriens* shouldn't be yet another thing that piles up. Rather, I want you to see it as an invitation to quiet time with the Lord. When you approach it with the right attitude, you never really "fall behind" on *Oriens*.

One of the Devil's most successful temptations is to distract people for a day or two so they don't remember to pick up *Oriens*. Then when they finally remember to pray, the enemy whispers, "Oh well, you failed. You might as well give up now. You could try again next year." You wouldn't believe how many people fall for this little trick. There's also the daily trick: "I only have a few minutes now, so instead of praying, I'll focus on the things that are piling up, and wait to pray until I get some of those things done first." You can guess what happens next. That's right, you never catch up.

If you do fall a few days behind, do this: Turn to today's date and pray that day's meditation as well as you can. You're all caught up! The goal is quality time with God, not getting every prayer prayed or making nice notes in your journal.

That having been said, the more you are able to open the book each day, the more you will benefit from the pilgrimage. Any prayer time in a day, however small, is a victory. Even just opening the book before bed and reading the Scripture passage for that day is a victory. We are on a prayer pilgrimage. If you just keep walking, even baby steps will eventually get you to your destination.

Grace of the Week: This week we will continue through the days of the Christmas countdown. Let us open our hearts to our King, who humbled himself to free all men and women from sin, Satan, and death. Ask God for a deeper awareness of the presence of his Emmanuel, God-with-us, in your daily life.

December 21 — Sunday
Fourth Sunday of Advent
Countdown to Christmas: 5

O Emmanuel, our King and Giver of Law:
come to save us, Lord our God!

Preparation: *Come, Holy Spirit, enlighten the eyes of my heart.* Be present to the God who is always present to you. Call to mind his loving care for you and spend the first minute of your prayer just resting in the free, unearned gift of loving and being loved. Let gratitude rise in your heart.

Set the Scene: Ask God for a deeper awareness of the presence of his Emmanuel, God-with-us, in your daily life, that your heart might leap for joy. Read the passage through and picture the scene. Tradition identifies this location as a town called Ein Karem, a hill town about five miles to the west of Jerusalem and about ninety miles from Nazareth. Elizabeth is already six months pregnant. Mary hasn't started to show yet.

LUKE 1:39–45 (LECTIONARY)

Mary set out
and traveled to the hill country in haste
to a town of Judah,
where she entered the house of Zechariah
and greeted Elizabeth.
When Elizabeth heard Mary's greeting,
the infant leaped in her womb,
and Elizabeth, filled with the Holy Spirit,
cried out in a loud voice and said,
"Blessed are you among women,
and blessed is the fruit of your womb.
And how does this happen to me,

> that the mother of my Lord should come to me?
> For at the moment the sound of your greeting reached
>   my ears,
> the infant in my womb leaped for joy.
> Blessed are you who believed
> that what was spoken to you by the Lord
> would be fulfilled."

Action! *Emmanuel* means "God-with-us" (see Is 7:14; 8:10). How was God with Mary on her journey to visit Elizabeth? How does Elizabeth feel in the presence of her infant Lord? How is God with you right now?

Acknowledge: Christmas is a busy time for visiting and receiving visitors. Do your visitors bring the presence of Jesus to your home, or do they bring worries of being judged for a messy home? When you visit others, how do you bring Jesus with you to their home? When did you leap for joy at God's presence in your life? Read the passage a second time.

Relate: Let your thoughts and feelings rise to the surface. Speak to God what is in your heart.

Receive: How does God the Father view this scene? How does he gaze upon your home and your guests? How is God with you when you are visiting others? Receive whatever is in God's heart for you — his thoughts, feelings, desires. Read the passage a third time.

Respond: Converse with God in your heart. Then just savor the presence of Jesus for a minute or two before moving on.

SUGGESTIONS FOR JOURNALING
1. My heart leaped for joy when ...
2. I noticed God with me and he wanted me to know...
3. I ended prayer wanting ...
4. Prayer time gave me a new perspective about...
5. Is there a way I can "go in haste" to share with another the joy I am receiving through these Advent prayer times?

After you've journaled, close with a brief conversation with God giving thanks for your prayer experience. Then pray an Our Father.

December 22 — Monday
Countdown to Christmas: 4

O King of all nations and keystone of the Church:
come and save man,
whom you formed from the dust!

Preparation: *Come, Holy Spirit, enlighten the eyes of my heart.* Be present to the God who is always present to you. Call to mind his loving care for you and spend the first minute of your prayer just resting in the free, unearned gift of loving and being loved. Let gratitude rise in your heart.

Lectio: Ask in your own words for a deeper awareness of the presence of his Emmanuel, God-with-us, in your daily life. This Scripture is called the *Magnificat* (which is the first word of this passage in Latin). It is a hymn of praise to God who has been faithful to his promises from Abraham until today. This could very well be a song that the saints sing in heaven. Is there one word or phrase that you feel moved to focus on? Read the passage slowly and prayerfully.

LUKE 1:46–56 (LECTIONARY)
Mary said:

"My soul proclaims the greatness of the Lord;
my spirit rejoices in God my savior.
for he has looked upon his lowly servant.
From this day all generations will call me blessed:
the Almighty has done great things for me,
and holy is his Name.
He has mercy on those who fear him
in every generation.
He has shown the strength of his arm,
and has scattered the proud in their conceit.

*He has cast down the mighty from their thrones
and has lifted up the lowly.
He has filled the hungry with good things,
and the rich he has sent away empty.
He has come to the help of his servant Israel
for he remembered his promise of mercy,
the promise he made to our fathers,
to Abraham and his children forever."*

Mary remained with Elizabeth about three months and then returned to her home.

Meditatio: Have you noticed recent news stories where God was humbling the proud or lifting up the lowly? How has God done great things for you? Have you experienced his mercy, blessing, or strength? Or perhaps you feel lowly, humbled, someone who needs to be raised from the dust, and you are waiting for the king of all nations to come rescue you with the might of his arm. Reflect for a few minutes, or just focus on the word or phrase that speaks to you. Then read the passage again slowly.

Oratio: Speak to God what is on your heart and mind, your thoughts, feelings, and desires. When you are done speaking, read the passage one more time.

Contemplatio: Open your heart to receive what God wants to give you. Maybe it is a thought, a word, or a sense of peace. God is with you in this ordinary moment. Even his challenging words come with love. Rest in and savor his love for you. Be present. Be lowly.

SUGGESTIONS FOR JOURNALING
1. My favorite word or phrase was …
2. God fulfilled his promises to me when …
3. I rejoice in God my Savior when I recall …
4. The people and the world around me most need to hear …
5. Mary takes Jesus with her wherever she goes. How can I take Jesus with me on my journey today?

124 *December 22 — Monday*

After you've journaled, close with a brief conversation with God giving thanks for your prayer experience. Then close by reading today's Scripture one more time as a prayer of praise and thanksgiving.

December 23 — Tuesday
Countdown to Christmas: 3

O King of all nations and keystone of the Church:
come and save man,
whom you formed from the dust!

Preparation: *Come, Holy Spirit, enlighten the eyes of my heart.* Be present to the God who is always present to you. Call to mind his loving care for you and spend the first minute of your prayer just resting in the free, unearned gift of loving and being loved. Let gratitude rise in your heart.

Set the Scene: Ask God in your own words for a deeper awareness of the presence of his Emmanuel, God-with-us, in your daily life. It's easy to imagine Elizabeth's neighbors and relatives gathering around to celebrate the birth of a healthy baby boy. The circumcision was like a baptism party. The name *John* means "God is gracious." Set the scene in your imagination. Populate it with villagers.

LUKE 1:57–66 (LECTIONARY)
When the time arrived for Elizabeth to have her child
she gave birth to a son.
Her neighbors and relatives heard
that the Lord had shown his great mercy toward her,
and they rejoiced with her.
When they came on the eighth day to circumcise the child,
they were going to call him Zechariah after his father,
but his mother said in reply,
"No. He will be called John."
But they answered her,
"There is no one among your relatives who has this name."
So they made signs, asking his father what he wished him

> to be called.
> He asked for a tablet and wrote, "John is his name,"
> and all were amazed.
> Immediately his mouth was opened, his tongue freed,
> and he spoke blessing God.
> Then fear came upon all their neighbors,
> and all these matters were discussed
> throughout the hill country of Judea.
> All who heard these things took them to heart, saying,
> "What, then, will this child be?
> For surely the hand of the Lord was with him."

Action! What was the look on Zechariah's face when he first met his son? It's easy to imagine that Mary was with Elizabeth as she gave birth. Eight days later, guests are coming for the circumcision party. Picture how excited the neighbors are as they all come together. Zachariah is only a silent participant — imagine the look on his face as he welcomes his guests. Imagine the look on everyone's face when suddenly he can speak again! Place yourself within the crowd.

Acknowledge: How do you feel at the birth of this child who will prepare the way for the *king of all nations and keystone of the Church*? What thoughts and feelings rise in your heart? Read the passage a second time.

Relate: God the Father is also a silent participant, gazing at the scene with love. Speak to God what is in your heart. If you have a hard time relating to God the Father, find Mary among the crowd of guests and speak to her.

Receive: Read the passage a third time and receive whatever is in God's heart for you — his thoughts, feelings, desires. Does your heavenly Father look at you like Zechariah looked at his son, John?

Respond: Let the Father look at you and look back at him. Just savor the joy of being your Father's child for a few minutes before moving on.

SUGGESTIONS FOR JOURNALING
1. I was surprised by …
2. Zechariah teaches me …
3. The Father seemed to be saying to me …
4. When do I feel tongue-tied, or when do I find it hard to speak to God? Or was there something today that I had a hard time receiving and accepting?
5. I ended prayer wanting …

128 *December 23 — Tuesday*

After you've journaled, close with a brief conversation with God giving thanks for your prayer experience. Then pray an Our Father.

December 24 — Wednesday
Countdown to Christmas: 2

O Radiant Dawn, splendor of eternal light, sun of justice:
come and shine on those who dwell in darkness
and in the shadow of death.

Preparation: *Come, Holy Spirit, enlighten the eyes of my heart.* Be present to the God who is always present to you. Call to mind his loving care for you and spend the first minute of your prayer just resting in the free, unearned gift of loving and being loved. Let gratitude rise in your heart.

Lectio: Ask God in your own words for a deeper awareness of the presence of his Emmanuel, God-with-us, in your daily life. Zechariah hasn't spoken for nine months — and now he has a lot to say! He proclaims that this child will brighten all the world and bring a freedom far greater than the Israelites experienced as they left Egypt. Read this passage slowly and prayerfully. Is there a word or phrase that speaks to you most strongly?

LUKE 1:67–79 (LECTIONARY)

Zechariah his father, filled with the Holy Spirit, prophesied, saying:

"Blessed be the Lord, the God of Israel;
for he has come to his people and set them free.
He has raised up for us a mighty Savior,
born of the house of his servant David.
Through his prophets he promised of old
that he would save us from our enemies,
from the hands of all who hate us.
He promised to show mercy to our fathers
and to remember his holy covenant.
This was the oath he swore to our father Abraham:

> to set us free from the hand of our enemies,
> free to worship him without fear,
> holy and righteous in his sight
> all the days of our life.
> You, my child, shall be called the prophet of the Most High,
> for you will go before the Lord to prepare his way,
> to give his people knowledge of salvation
> by the forgiveness of their sins.
> In the tender compassion of our God
> the dawn from on high shall break upon us,
> to shine on those who dwell in darkness and the shadow
>   of death,
> and to guide our feet into the way of peace."

Meditatio: *O Radiant Dawn!* The dawn from on high that shall break upon us. You guessed it, that is the word *Oriens*. With this being the day before Christmas, it is as though the dawn is just starting to peek out over the hills. Have you felt God's light shining more brightly these last twenty-seven days? Has God been guiding your feet into the way of peace?

Oratio: Read the passage again, or maybe just the part that speaks to you. What do you want to say to God, with the birth of his Son so close at hand? Speak to God what is on your heart and mind.

Contemplatio: Read the passage one more time. Open your heart to receive what God wants to give you. God loves every child like an only child. Rest in and savor his love for you. Let the dawn from on high shine upon you. Bask in the light of God's love for a few minutes before moving on.

SUGGESTIONS FOR JOURNALING

1. God has set me free from …
2. I experienced the forgiveness of sins in a personal way when …
3. I feel the light of God shining in my heart when …
4. God's love feels like …
5. I need patience as I wait for …

After you've journaled, close with a brief conversation with God giving thanks for your prayer experience. Then pray an Our Father.

Announcement of the Birth of Christ from the Roman Martyrology

The text below, taken from the Roman Martyrology, presents the birth of Jesus as one would announce the birth of a king or emperor. The announcement is recited or chanted on December 24, during the celebration of the Liturgy of the Hours or before the Christmas Mass during the Night.

> The Twenty-fifth Day of December,
> when ages beyond number had run their course
> > from the creation of the world,
> when God in the beginning created heaven and earth,
> and formed man in his own likeness;
> when century upon century had passed
> since the Almighty set his bow in the clouds after the Great Flood,
> as a sign of covenant and peace;
> in the twenty-first century since Abraham, our father in faith,
> came out of Ur of the Chaldees;
> in the thirteenth century since the People of Israel were led by Moses
> in the Exodus from Egypt;
> around the thousandth year since David was anointed King;
> in the sixty-fifth week of the prophecy of Daniel;
> in the one hundred and ninety-fourth Olympiad;
> in the year seven hundred and fifty-two
> since the foundation of the City of Rome;
> in the forty-second year of the reign of Caesar Octavian Augustus,
> the whole world being at peace,
>
> JESUS CHRIST, eternal God and Son of the eternal Father,
> desiring to consecrate the world by his most loving presence,
> was conceived by the Holy Spirit,

and when nine months had passed since his conception,
was born of the Virgin Mary in Bethlehem of Judah, and was made man:

The Nativity of Our Lord Jesus Christ according to the flesh.
(Appendix I of the Roman Missal, 3rd ed.)

December 25 — Thursday
The Nativity of Our Lord Jesus Christ

The feast of Christmas is too big to fit into one day. For eight days we celebrate the long-awaited radiant Dawn, the Sun of Justice and King all nations who is Christ the Lord. I tell schoolchildren that the octave of Christmas means you have to eat Christmas treats every day for eight days. The Gloria is sung at Mass for all eight days of the octave. Several of these days are special feast days dedicated to particular saints.

During the octave, swap out the purple and pink candles on your Advent wreath for white candles. Light them when you eat your family meals and sing a Christmas carol together each time. And keep making time for your pilgrimage! We've come through Advent and have only begun to journey through Christmas.

Preparation: *Come, Holy Spirit, enlighten the eyes of my heart.* Be present to the God who is always present to you. Call to mind his loving care for you and spend the first minute of your prayer just resting in the free, unearned gift of loving and being loved. Let gratitude rise in your heart.

Set the Scene: Ask God in your own words for a deeper awareness of the presence of his Emmanuel, God-with-us, in your daily life. We like to think of the Nativity as something easy, peaceful, and cozy. We are so used to the idyllic stable with happy angels floating around it. But our Gospel implies crowds thronging to fulfill Caesar's decree, a long journey on dusty roads with a very pregnant woman, and the Holy Family finding themselves homeless at the most inopportune time. Read through the Gospel to set the scene in your imagination.

LUKE 2:1-14 MASS DURING THE NIGHT (LECTIONARY)
LUKE 2:15-20 MASS AT DAWN (LECTIONARY)
In those days a decree went out from Caesar Augustus that the whole world should be enrolled.

*This was the first enrollment,
when Quirinius was governor of Syria.
So all went to be enrolled, each to his own town.
And Joseph too went up from Galilee from the town of Nazareth
to Judea, to the city of David that is called Bethlehem,
because he was of the house and family of David,
to be enrolled with Mary, his betrothed, who was with child.
While they were there,
the time came for her to have her child,
and she gave birth to her firstborn son.
She wrapped him in swaddling clothes and laid him in a manger,
because there was no room for them in the inn.*

*Now there were shepherds in that region living in the fields
and keeping the night watch over their flock.
The angel of the Lord appeared to them
and the glory of the Lord shone around them,
and they were struck with great fear.
The angel said to them,
"Do not be afraid;
for behold, I proclaim to you good news of great joy
that will be for all the people.
For today in the city of David
a savior has been born for you who is Christ and Lord.
And this will be a sign for you:
you will find an infant wrapped in swaddling clothes
and lying in a manger."
And suddenly there was a multitude of the heavenly host with the angel,
praising God and saying:
"Glory to God in the highest
and on earth peace to those on whom his favor rests."*

*When the angels went away from them to heaven,
the shepherds said to one another,
"Let us go, then, to Bethlehem
to see this thing that has taken place,
which the Lord has made known to us."
So they went in haste and found Mary and Joseph,
and the infant lying in the manger.
When they saw this,
they made known the message
that had been told them about this child.
All who heard it were amazed
by what had been told them by the shepherds.
And Mary kept all these things,
reflecting on them in her heart.
Then the shepherds returned,
glorifying and praising God
for all they had heard and seen,
just as it had been told to them.*

Action! Picture Joseph and a very pregnant Mary trying to trust God as they are suddenly forced by world events to make a long journey to Bethlehem. How were they feeling? God provides a nice, soft bed for his son, though not in the way one might have expected. The shepherds were not expecting heavenly visitors that cold December night. What is in their hearts as they gaze at the infant Savior? Where do you find yourself in this scene?

Acknowledge: Shepherds tended to have a bad reputation in the ancient world (something like the suspicion with which gypsies have been seen in Europe). Shepherds in those days were not accepted as valid witnesses for a court case. God has, in fact, made the Good News known precisely to the people that society mistrusts. God is "lifting up the lowly" as those on the periphery of society are suddenly given a front row seat to God fulfilling his promise of mercy. What is in Mary's heart? Joseph's heart? The hearts of the shepherds? Your heart? Read the passage a second time.

Relate: Perhaps you can ask Mary to let you hold her child. What do you feel in your heart as you contemplate the Savior? Speak to God what is in your heart.

Receive: Receive whatever is in God's heart for you. Read the passage a third time.

Respond: Just savor the joy of holding the Son and being held by the Father for a little while. Let God the Father gaze at you as you gaze on the face of his son.

SUGGESTIONS FOR JOURNALING
1. The glory of the Lord shone in my Christmas celebration when …
2. I felt God's love most strongly …
3. What does it mean to say that Jesus was born for me?
4. The Father seemed to be saying to me …
5. I was surprised by …
6. My heart rested when …
7. Christmas means to me …
8. On the first day of Christmas, my True Love gave to me …

Spend a minute thanking Jesus for being God-with-you in your prayer experience today, then close with an Our Father.

December 26 — Friday
Second Day in the Octave of Christmas

SAINT STEPHEN, DEACON AND MARTYR

Stephen was one of seven men chosen to be the first deacons of the infant church (see Acts 6:1–6). They were ordained specifically to take over the Church's care for the widows, a sign that charity for the needy is an essential part of the Gospel. He did great wonders and signs and preached the Gospel with so much wisdom that his opponents were confounded. They falsely accused him of blasphemy, and a mob stoned him to death (6:8—8:1). He is the first in a long line of faithful servants who gave their lives in witness to the true King. This feast reminds us that Jesus was born into time so that Stephen, and all of us, could be born into eternity.

Preparation: *Come, Holy Spirit, enlighten the eyes of my heart.* Be present to the God who is always present to you. Call to mind his loving care for you and spend the first minute of your prayer just resting in the free, unearned gift of loving and being loved. Let gratitude rise in your heart.

Set the Scene: Ask God in your own words for a deeper awareness of the presence of his Emmanuel, God-with-us, in your daily life. Hopefully we are still glowing with the light of the Nativity scene. We want the peace and joy of baby Jesus to enter more deeply into our hearts. The Church has long celebrated the feast of the first martyr the day after the birthday of Jesus. His martyrdom happens not too long after Jesus' resurrection and the feast of Pentecost. The young Christian Church has been spreading rapidly. Stephen is an effective apologist, meaning that he explains or defends the truths of the Faith. He is also filled with the Holy Spirit; the "signs and wonders" the Bible mentions him working are most likely miracles of healing and exorcism. His opponents try to prove him wrong through philosophical and theological debates, but the debate only proves him more right. They resort to violence. Read the passage and picture the scene in your mind.

ACTS 6:8–10; 7:54–59 (LECTIONARY)

Stephen, filled with grace and power,
was working great wonders and signs among the people.
Certain members of the so-called Synagogue of Freedmen,
Cyrenians, and Alexandrians,
and people from Cilicia and Asia,
came forward and debated with Stephen,
but they could not withstand the wisdom and the spirit with which he spoke.

When they heard this, they were infuriated,
and they ground their teeth at him.
But he, filled with the Holy Spirit,
looked up intently to heaven
and saw the glory of God and Jesus standing at the right hand of God,
and he said,
"Behold, I see the heavens opened and the Son of Man standing at the right hand of God."
But they cried out in a loud voice, covered their ears,
and rushed upon him together.
They threw him out of the city, and began to stone him.
The witnesses laid down their cloaks
at the feet of a young man named Saul.
As they were stoning Stephen, he called out
"Lord Jesus, receive my spirit."

Action! As the whirlwind of anger and hatred unfolds around him, focus on the peace in Stephen's heart. Acts 6:15 says, "All those who sat in the Sanhedrin looked intently at him and saw that his face was like the face of an angel." The heavens are opened, and Stephen sees Jesus himself in glory. He ends his life in imitation of Jesus' death on the cross. Like Jesus' own death, the death of Stephen is a story of redemption. The Saul who appears at the end of today's reading will appear again on January 25.

Acknowledge: Place yourself in the scene. Focus on the part that speaks to you. What gives Stephen the strength to remain faithful to Christ even in the midst of hatred and violence? Perhaps you love the Christ Child, but would you die for him? Do you trust that the Holy Spirit would give you the words to respond to your enemies and the grace to be faithful until death? Read the passage a second time.

Relate: The same Jesus who appeared to Stephen standing at the right hand of God is now standing with you. Turn to him. Share with him honestly what is on your heart, without fear of "saying the wrong thing" or being judged. Jesus already knows what you are thinking, but he's waiting for you to turn to him.

Receive: Read the passage a third time. Open your heart to how Jesus wants to respond to you — a word, a phrase, or just his silent, loving presence. Spend a few minutes in the presence of the Almighty who became a little child.

Respond: You, too, are valuable to God, as Stephen was valuable to him. Savor the light of the Holy Spirit shining on your heart and respond to whatever God is giving you. Spend a minute or two in silent conversation before moving on.

SUGGESTIONS FOR JOURNALING
1. I never realized that …
2. I see a new connection between Christmas and the feast of Stephen …
3. My strongest thought, feeling, or desire was …
4. Jesus gave me the gift of …
5. I ended prayer with a new appreciation of the Christmas story …
6. On the second day of Christmas, my True Love gave to me …

142 *December 26 — Friday*

After you've journaled, thank God for his presence with you and his love for you in today's prayer time. Join with Stephen and all the members of God's heavenly family as you pray an Our Father.

December 27 — Saturday
Third Day in the Octave of Christmas

SAINT JOHN, APOSTLE AND EVANGELIST, MEMORIAL
Born in Bethsaida on the Sea of Galilee, the brother of James and a fisherman by trade, John was called to follow Jesus while mending his nets (see Mk 1:19–20). Along with his brother James and fellow fisherman Peter, he was present at the Transfiguration of the Lord (Mk 9:2–8). The Gospel that bears his name refers to him only as "the beloved disciple." He was the one who reclined next to Jesus at the Last Supper (Jn 13:23) and stood at the foot of the cross as Jesus died. Jesus entrusted his mother to John's care (Jn 19:26–27). He wrote the fourth Gospel, three epistles, and is credited with the Book of Revelation. He was the only apostle not to be martyred. Tradition holds that he was miraculously preserved from attempts, including a chalice of poisoned wine, which is why the medieval Church included a blessing of wine on his feast day. He died in exile on the island of Patmos. Many scholars believe that he wants every Christian to see himself or herself as "the beloved disciple." Do you see yourself this way?

REVIEW
Preparation: *Come, Holy Spirit, enlighten the eyes of my heart.* Call to mind God's loving care for you and spend the first minute of your prayer just resting in the free, unearned gift of loving and being loved. Let gratitude rise in your heart.

Grace for the Day: What is the desire of your heart? Try to notice what you most deeply desire. Then share it with God in your own words, being confident that he loves you and wants to give you every blessing.

Week in Review: Flip back through your past week's journal entries. As you do, notice what emerged in the conversation. Here are some questions to help you:

December 27 — Saturday

1. Where did I notice God, and what was he doing or saying?
2. How did I respond to what God was doing?
3. I felt God's love most strongly when …
4. I found myself struggling with …
5. I'm grateful for …
6. On the third day of Christmas, my True Love gave to me …

_____
_____
_____
_____
_____
_____
_____
_____
_____
_____
_____

Now go back to your journal entries from the First Sunday of Advent and then the last few Saturday reviews.

1. What did I desire as I began this journey? Have those desires grown or changed in some way?
2. Do I notice a particular theme that has been emerging on my Advent pilgrimage?
3. Do I have recurring fears or struggles that Jesus is wanting

to address with me?
4. This Christmas, God has given me the gift of …
5. How has this Advent journey changed me?
6. My strongest sense, image, moment or experience of God's loving presence was …

Acknowledge what you have been experiencing. **Relate** it to him. **Receive** what he wants to give you. **Respond** to him. Then savor that image of God's loving presence and rest there for a minute or two. Close with an Our Father.

Week Five

Well Begun Is Half Done

Saint Ignatius is the "father" of the thirty-day silent retreat. He told retreatants to begin each prayer time by "pausing for the space of an Our Father and considering how God our Lord looks upon us." I wasn't sure how to do that. I tried various images of God's love, but it never really clicked for me, nor for the people I directed on retreats. I didn't want to let it go, though. If we don't start prayer by realizing we are not alone, we might never actually get to conversation with God. Prayer will become nothing more than a conversation with myself, as I read spiritual things and think up spiritual thoughts and goals for myself.

While writing this book, I toyed with a variety of different ways to start the prayer time. I eventually realized that once you have had an experience of God's loving care for you, you can keep "recycling" that experience by starting your next day from that place. Saint Ignatius wasn't inviting us to invent how God might look at us, but rather to return to a place, prayer image, or Scripture passage where we have encountered God's love.

God never stops loving us. The sun will stop shining before God stops loving you. But we don't always feel his love. Today I might feel burdened, distracted, lost, confused, or even abandoned. However, God and I have a history together; I have experienced his loving care in the past, and I am sure to experience it again in the future. So, I begin my prayer by remembering a time that I felt particularly loved, blessed, and cared for. This helps me enter back into that moment and begin my prayer from a place of gratitude. If you have never had an experience of God's love or you find it hard to return to that place, you can use an icon or favorite image of Jesus such as Divine Mercy or the Good Shepherd. It's not so important that you feel loved in this moment. It's most important that you realize that, regardless of how you feel, you are in fact seen and known and loved right now in this moment.

Before we finish our prayer time, we should end with gratitude. When we realize what God has done for us, how he has loved us faithfully and sent his Son to die for us, we cannot help but feel grateful. Gratitude is the antidote to anger, the antithesis of a consumer mentality, and the right attitude of a disciple. Our prayer should begin and end with gratitude.

Mother Church has the same idea when we traditionally pray both a grace before meals and a grace after meals. However meager our meals may be, they are a gift from God, and we need to begin and end with gratitude. The Church's Morning Prayer is called "Morning Praises" (*laudes*) to begin our day with gratitude. Night Prayer ends with a hymn to Our Lady, an act of gratitude for her maternal care. The word *Eucharist* means "thanksgiving," as we begin and end our week with gratitude. Every Saturday after I review my week, I write down the top things I am grateful for and collect them in a gratitude jar. At the end of the year, I dump out the jar and sift through all my blessings. Our meals, prayer time, days, weeks, and years should begin and end with gratitude.

Grace of the Week: We will journey through the end of 2025 and begin our new year with Mary, the Mother of God. She received God's only-begotten Son in her womb and formed his humanity. For our grace this week, we will ask our Father to help us experience and live more deeply our true identity as beloved children of God.

December 28 — Sunday
The Holy Family of Jesus, Mary, and Joseph

Preparation: *Come, Holy Spirit, enlighten the eyes of my heart.* Be present to the God who is always present to you. Call to mind his loving care for you and spend the first minute of your prayer just resting in the free, unearned gift of loving and being loved. Let gratitude rise in your heart.

Set the Scene: Ask God in our own words to help you experience and live more deeply your true identity as a beloved child of God. This feast day is celebrated on the Sunday between Christmas and New Year's. It helps us to take a step back from the manger itself and see more clearly the human family which welcomed Jesus and was made holy by his presence. As Jesus reveals what God intended when he created man, so the holy family helps us to see what God intended with the family. Picture the scene in your mind as you read the passage.

MATTHEW 2:13–15, 19–23 (LECTIONARY)

When the magi had departed, behold,
the angel of the Lord appeared to Joseph in a dream and said,
"Rise, take the child and his mother, flee to Egypt,
and stay there until I tell you.
Herod is going to search for the child to destroy him."
Joseph rose and took the child and his mother by night
and departed for Egypt.
He stayed there until the death of Herod,
that what the Lord had said through the prophet might be fulfilled,
Out of Egypt I called my son.

When Herod had died, behold,
the angel of the Lord appeared in a dream

> to Joseph in Egypt and said,
> "Rise, take the child and his mother and go to the land
>   of Israel,
> for those who sought the child's life are dead."
> He rose, took the child and his mother,
> and went to the land of Israel.
> But when he heard that Archelaus was ruling over Judea
> in place of his father Herod,
> he was afraid to go back there.
> And because he had been warned in a dream,
> he departed for the region of Galilee.
> He went and dwelt in a town called Nazareth,
> so that what had been spoken through the prophets
>   might be fulfilled,
> He shall be called a Nazorean.

Action! In the early days of the Jewish people, Egypt was a superpower. Guided by Joseph's dreams, Israel and his sons found refuge there from a famine (see Gn 46). Egypt then enslaved the Jewish people and became a symbol for the powers of the world that oppose and persecute God's children. In Jesus' day, Egypt and Israel were at peace with each other as they were both dominated by Rome. A thriving community of expat Jews would have made it an attractive locale to escape from the clutches of King Herod. Picture Joseph's unquestioning, prompt obedience to God's messages. How does Mary respond? How does the baby Jesus respond? What was it like to live in Egypt, then Nazareth? Use your imagination.

Acknowledge: My family moved a number of times as I was growing up. Being uprooted and replanted was sometimes a traumatic experience. However, I believe these moves were, in fact, orchestrated by God's hand. There were always blessings waiting for us, and the experiences helped to shape the person I am today. What experiences from your life connect with the experience of the Holy Family? How has God turned difficulties and even traumas into blessings in your life? Read the passage again and notice what stirs inside of you.

Relate: Joseph is worried for the family's safety when he finds that Herod's son is now sitting on his father's throne. He trusts in God and discovers that God shares his concerns and has an answer for him. Share your concerns with God. Be open and honest about what has been stirred up within you.

Receive: Do you have a sense of how God receives what you have shared with him? Do you have a sense of how God responds to your concerns? Sometimes you will notice an immediate response such as a word, Scripture passage, or song lyrics that come to mind. Other times you will receive a sense of peace, that God hears you and values what you have to say. Perhaps the response will come later in the form of a message from a friend or even a dream! God doesn't stop talking just because our prayer time is over. But be open to receive whatever he wants to give you in this moment. Read the passage a third time.

Respond: Have a conversation with God or thank him for whatever it is you have received through this prayer time. Savor his loving presence with you for a few minutes before moving on.

SUGGESTIONS FOR JOURNALING
1. The Holy Family's experience resonated with my experience of …
2. I felt God calling me and guiding me when …
3. My strongest thought, feeling, or desire was …
4. I sensed that God wanted me to know …
5. I feel called to a new way of thinking, living, or acting …
6. I desire for my family …
7. On the fourth day of Christmas, my True Love gave to me …

154 *December 28 — Sunday*

After you've journaled, spend a final minute thanking God for his presence in today's prayer experience, then pray an Our Father.

December 29 — Monday
Fifth Day in the Octave of Christmas

ST. THOMAS BECKET, BISHOP AND MARTYR

Thomas Becket was born in London in 1118. A cleric of the diocese of Canterbury, he became chancellor to King Henry II and took a leading part in a military expedition against the French. When the archbishop died, Thomas was chosen as his replacement. Perhaps Henry wanted "his man" to be chief cleric in England. However, Thomas took his new responsibilities very seriously and began a life of penance and simplicity. He led a protracted defense of the Church's independence from the crown, which resulted in six years of exile. On this day in 1170, knights and a band of armed men slew him in his church. King Henry did public penance for this crime.

Preparation: *Come, Holy Spirit, enlighten the eyes of my heart.* Be present to the God who is always present to you. Call to mind his loving care for you and spend the first minute of your prayer just resting in the free, unearned gift of loving and being loved. Let gratitude rise in your heart.

Lectio: Ask God in our own words to help you experience and live more deeply your true identity as a beloved child of God. We will take a look again at the goodness of God, this time by using the Psalm that will be read at daily Mass the next three days. The ancients saw the order, perfection, and dependability of the heavens as a sign of what God was like. We tend to blame God for the evil in the world. Some people even doubt God exists because they see so much evil. However, Scripture makes it clear that evil arises from the heart of man when he is tricked by the world, the flesh, and the Devil. God himself is good and the source of all goodness. Let us praise God for his goodness, justice, and constancy. Perhaps use your imagination to picture the heavenly cosmos as you read this passage.

PSALM 96:1–2A, 2B–3, 5B–6, 7–8A, 8B–9, 10, 11–12, 13 (LECTIONARY — DECEMBER 29, 30, 31)

Sing to the LORD a new song;
sing to the LORD, all you lands.
Sing to the LORD, bless his name;

Announce his salvation, day after day.
Tell his glory among the nations;
among all peoples, his wondrous deeds.

The LORD made the heavens.
Splendor and majesty go before him;
power and grandeur are in his sanctuary.

Give to the LORD, you families of nations,
give to the LORD glory and praise;
give to the LORD the glory due his name!

Bring gifts, and enter his courts;
worship the LORD in holy attire.
Tremble before him, all the earth.

Say among the nations: The LORD is king.
He has made the world firm, not to be moved;
he governs the peoples with equity.

Let the heavens be glad and the earth rejoice;
let the sea and what fills it resound;
let the plains be joyful and all that is in them!
Then let all the trees of the forest exult before the LORD.

The LORD comes,
he comes to rule the earth.
He shall rule the world with justice
and the peoples with his constancy.

Meditatio: Man is a steward of God's creation, but his stewardship will not last forever. God himself will one day return to cast out evil and darkness and to rule the world with justice and equity. The earth and all creation are excited for this moment. How have you experienced God's goodness in your own life? How have you experienced God's goodness through your *Oriens* pilgrimage this year?

Oratio: Saint Paul says, "We know that all creation is groaning in labor pains even until now; and not only that, but we ourselves, who have the firstfruits of the Spirit, we also groan within ourselves as we wait for adoption, the redemption of our bodies" (Rom 8:22–23). The Lord will come to rule the earth. His Second Coming is already near. Do you tremble with excitement, or with fear? Where in your life, or in your world, are you groaning as you wait to experience God's justice and equity? Read the passage a second time, then speak to God about these places that need his loving touch.

Contemplatio: Read the passage a third time, slowly and prayerfully. As you do, receive God's response to your words. What is in God's heart for you? What does God long to give you? How will he make things right for you? Rejoice that he hears you, and then spend a few minutes in prayerful communion with God before moving on.

SUGGESTIONS FOR JOURNALING

1. Gazing at the heavens, the sea, the plains, and the trees, I am reminded that …
2. The word or phrase that most spoke to me today was …
3. What am I groaning for?
4. What is God desiring to give me? What is he waiting for?
5. I ended prayer with a deeper sense that …
6. On the fifth day of Christmas, my True Love gave to me …

158 *December 29 — Monday*

After you've journaled, spend a moment thanking God for his constancy in your life, then end with an Our Father.

December 30 — Tuesday
Sixth Day in the Octave of Christmas

Preparation: *Come, Holy Spirit, enlighten the eyes of my heart.* Be present to the God who is always present to you. Call to mind his loving care for you and spend the first minute of your prayer just resting in the free, unearned gift of loving and being loved. Let gratitude rise in your heart.

Lectio: Ask God in your own words to help you experience and live more deeply your true identity as a beloved child of God. The letters of Saint John are commonly thought to have been written after he finished his Gospel. He wants to drive home some simple truths and avoid the temptation to overly spiritualize the Christian message, ignoring or denying the true humanity of Jesus and his real presence in history. The letter is simple and repetitive. Perhaps picture an old man making the same simple but profound points again and again. His listeners nod with knowing winks; they've heard it all a thousand times before. But has it really sunk in? Perhaps John can see that their hearts do not fully accept and remain in God's love for them. Read the passage slowly and prayerfully.

1 JOHN 2:12–17 (LECTIONARY)
I am writing to you, children,
because your sins have been forgiven for his name's sake.

I am writing to you, fathers,
because you know him who is from the beginning.

I am writing to you, young men,
because you have conquered the Evil One.

I write to you, children,
because you know the Father.

I write to you, fathers,
because you know him who is from the beginning.

I write to you, young men,
because you are strong and the word of God remains in you,
and you have conquered the Evil One.

Do not love the world or the things of the world.
If anyone loves the world, the love of the Father is not in him.
For all that is in the world,
sensual lust, enticement for the eyes, and a pretentious life,
is not from the Father but is from the world.
Yet the world and its enticement are passing away.
But whoever does the will of God remains forever.

Meditatio: "Enticements" describes very well all manner of Christmas commercials. They completely grab our focus and attention, then disappear so suddenly after Christmas Day. "Yet the world and its enticement are passing away." Do you want to constantly chase after enticements, or do you want to pursue the things that will last? Reflect on the things that took your focus and attention in the weeks leading up to Christmas. Did you focus on loving God and doing the will of God?

Oratio: You have been forgiven, you have conquered the Evil One, and you know him who is from the beginning. Speak to the one whose word remains in you. Read the passage a second time, then speak to God from your heart. Tell him your fears and worries and the desire of your heart.

Contemplatio: Once you are done speaking, read the passage one more time with an attitude of receiving. Be open to whatever God wants to give you. Then rest and remain in his loving care for you for a few minutes.

SUGGESTIONS FOR JOURNALING
1. I have experienced conquering the Evil One when …
2. The things of this world that most entice me are …
3. Doing the will of God feels like …
4. I ended prayer with a deeper sense that …
5. On the sixth day of Christmas, my True Love gave to me …

After you've journaled, spend a moment thanking God for the blessings of this prayer time today, then end with an Our Father.

December 31 — Wednesday
Seventh Day in the Octave of Christmas

Preparation: *Come, Holy Spirit, enlighten the eyes of my heart.* Be present to the God who is always present to you. Call to mind his loving care for you and spend the first minute of your prayer just resting in the free, unearned gift of loving and being loved. Let gratitude rise in your heart.

Lectio: Ask God in your own words to help you experience and live more deeply your true identity as a beloved child of God. Apparently, many people who once followed the Gospel are now preaching and teaching things that are contrary to the true Christian faith. It makes Saint John very sad, and he is also concerned with how their desertion might influence the rest of the Christian community. Read the passage slowly and prayerfully.

1 JOHN 2:18-21

Children, it is the last hour; and just as you heard that the antichrist was coming, so now many antichrists have appeared. Thus we know this is the last hour. They went out from us, but they were not really of our number; if they had been, they would have remained with us. Their desertion shows that none of them was of our number. But you have the anointing that comes from the holy one, and you all have knowledge. I write to you not because you do not know the truth but because you do, and because every lie is alien to the truth.

Meditatio: Many of us know friends, family members, coworkers, and neighbors who once seemed very faithful, but now no longer attend church. Did their attitude toward religion affect in any way your experience of Christmas? Are you able to draw from the "anointing that comes from the holy one" (the Holy Spirit)? Do you sometimes question the truth of the knowledge you have received from the Church and from your *Oriens* experience?

Oratio: Saint John sees a connection between our individual fellowship (communion) with the Father and our fellowship with one another. Those who do the Father's will and remain in his love will also love one another as brothers and sisters. Those who walk away from the community also reveal their lack of true communion with the Father. Read the passage a second time, then speak to God from your heart. Talk to him about the struggles you experience as you try to remain in a world with many Antichrists.

Contemplatio: Once you are done speaking, read the passage one more time with an attitude of receiving whatever God wants to say to you. Communion with God is closer than we often think. Receive his loving presence in whatever way you can. Then rest in the truth of God's love for you.

SUGGESTIONS FOR JOURNALING

1. When I am around people who no longer practice the Faith, it makes me think or feel …
2. The truth I have the hardest time accepting and living myself is …
3. God was with me, and he wanted me to know …
4. I ended prayer with a sense that …
5. On the seventh day of Christmas, my True Love gave to me …
6. Today is also New Year's Eve. How did God bless me in 2025? Perhaps flip back through the pictures on your phone and recall where you and God have been together.
7. As I look back on 2025 and then forward to next year, what is the one lesson or insight from this year that will change the way I live 2026? What concrete steps do I need to take to implement this change?

164 *December 31 — Wednesday*

After you've journaled, spend a moment in gratitude for the gift of this prayer time today, then end with an Our Father.

January 1 — Thursday
The Blessed Virgin Mary, the Mother of God

EIGHTH DAY IN THE OCTAVE OF CHRISTMAS

Preparation: *Come, Holy Spirit, enlighten the eyes of my heart.* Be present to the God who is always present to you. Call to mind his loving care for you and spend the first minute of your prayer just resting in the free, unearned gift of loving and being loved. Let gratitude rise in your heart.

Lectio: Ask God in our own words to help you experience and live more deeply your true identity as a beloved child of God. The title of Mary as "Mother of God" officially entered the Church's vocabulary in AD 431 at the Council of Ephesus. Jesus is one Person with two distinct natures, a human nature and a divine nature. Since Mary was Jesus' mother, and Jesus is God, is it proper to call Mary the Mother of God? Nestorius, patriarch of Constantinople, argued that God has no mother, and so Mary should only be referred to as the Mother of Christ. Cyril, the patriarch of Alexandria, disagreed. The pope supported Cyril, and the emperor supported Nestorius. Approximately 250 bishops gathered in Ephesus for what became known as the Third Ecumenical Council. The bishops sided with Cyril against Nestorius. Jesus does have two distinct natures, but a mother gives birth to a person, not a nature. Mary is the mother of a Person who is God, and therefore Mary is the Mother of God. You may have never thought of this feast day as a topic that was once deeply controversial. Be prepared to think more deeply as you read today's Scripture passage slowly and prayerfully.

GALATIANS 4:4–7 (LECTIONARY)

> Brothers and sisters:
> When the fullness of time had come, God sent his Son,
> born of a woman, born under the law,
> to ransom those under the law,
> so that we might receive adoption as sons.

As proof that you are sons,
God sent the Spirit of his Son into our hearts,
crying out, "Abba, Father!"
So you are no longer a slave but a son,
and if a son then also an heir, through God.

Meditatio: By a kind of marvelous exchange, God has taken on humanity so that we can receive his divinity. In his 1881 book *The Prince and the Pauper*, Mark Twain imagines a poor orphan switching places with the heir to the throne of England. This is exactly how Saint Paul understands the Incarnation. Jesus has entered the world disguised as a beggar and offered to switch places with us. He dies the death of a wretched sinner, and we are welcomed into the kingdom of God. What thoughts and feelings arise inside of you as you imagine such unimaginable generosity, such incredibly divine mercy?

Oratio: Read the passage a second time. The very Mother of God, Mary herself, is but a poor and lowly handmaid whom God raised to the dignity of the Queen of Heaven. Now she intercedes for all God's children and helps them be worthy of their high calling. In a sense, Mary trains us for heaven. Ask Mary to help you truly accept your dignity as a child of God. Picture God himself as a kind, loving, and thoughtful Father. Speak to him from your heart. The Spirit will help you. If you get stuck with this image and find it hard to relate to God in this way, ask Mary to help you.

Contemplatio: What does it mean to God that you are his child and he is your Father? Read the passage a third time very slowly and allow these words to enter your heart. Receive whatever God wants to give you and then rest in your Father's love for you for a few minutes before moving on.

SUGGESTIONS FOR JOURNALING
1. I find it hard to accept the idea that …
2. My heart leapt for joy when …
3. My biggest obstacle to accepting the fatherhood of God is …
4. My heart rested when …

5. In this new year, my deepest desire is …
6. On the eighth day of Christmas, my True Love gave to me …

After you've journaled, close with a brief conversation with your Father and your Mother, Mary the Mother of God, giving thanks for your prayer experience. Then pray an Our Father from your heart, truly meaning each word of the prayer that Jesus himself taught God's children.

January 2 — Friday
Friday Before Epiphany

STS. BASIL THE GREAT AND GREGORY NAZIANZEN, BISHOPS AND DOCTORS OF THE CHURCH, MEMORIAL

Basil was a brilliant student from a Christian family in Cappadocia (present-day Turkey). He was on his way to a great career as a teacher when he resigned and went to found what was probably the first monastery in Asia Minor. He became an archbishop and a famous orator who preached to large crowds. When Saint Athanasius died, Basil inherited the defense of orthodoxy against the Arian heresy. He died at the age of forty-nine.

Gregory was also from Cappadocia. He and Basil became friends at school. He followed Basil into monastic life. A retiring and sensitive soul, he was drawn into the Arian conflict when Basil ordained him bishop and sent him to rescue a diocese that was slipping into Arianism. After Basil's death, Gregory became the first orthodox bishop of Constantinople in thirty years. His brilliant sermons on the Trinity won him the nickname "the Theologian." He hated all the conflict and finally retired to a quiet life of prayer, meditation, and writing. Both are honored as Doctors (teachers) of the Church.

Preparation: *Come, Holy Spirit, enlighten the eyes of my heart.* Be present to the God who is always present to you. Call to mind his loving care for you and spend the first minute of your prayer just resting in the free, unearned gift of loving and being loved. Let gratitude rise in your heart.

Lectio: Ask God for the grace to help you experience and live more deeply your true identity as a beloved child of God. Falling in love happens suddenly and often without warning. We suddenly realize we have been swept off our feet by beauty, truth, and goodness. Falling out of love happens slowly and sometimes imperceptibly. Little frustrations build up due to poor communication and lack of quality time together. Habits of isolation develop. We realize that the person we once loved has become a stranger to us. Love must be protected, nurtured, and cherished. Saint

John is concerned that we who are beloved by God might fall out of love with God. See the love that Saint John has for the people to whom he is writing this letter. Picture his deep desire for them to know that they are precious, beautiful, and loved beyond measure. Read the passage slowly and prayerfully.

1 JOHN 2:22–28

Who is the liar? Whoever denies that Jesus is the Christ. Whoever denies the Father and the Son, this is the antichrist. No one who denies the Son has the Father, but whoever confesses the Son has the Father as well.

Let what you heard from the beginning remain in you. If what you heard from the beginning remains in you, then you will remain in the Son and in the Father. And this is the promise that he made us: eternal life. I write you these things about those who would deceive you. As for you, the anointing that you received from him remains in you, so that you do not need anyone to teach you. But his anointing teaches you about everything and is true and not false; just as it taught you, remain in him.

And now, children, remain in him, so that when he appears we may have confidence and not be put to shame by him at his coming.

Meditatio: "The anointing you received from him" refers to the Holy Spirit given at our baptism and again in the Sacrament of Confirmation. You cannot lose the Sacrament, but you can lose touch with the Holy Spirit. Have the time, effort, and energy you once put into prayer begun to wane? Are you finding yourself slipping into old habits again? What would you have to do, or to give up doing, to remain in the Son and in the Father, and to have confidence and not be put to shame at his coming?

Oratio: The Holy Spirit is with you. He will help you to know what it is that you most deeply desire. "Draw near to God, and he will draw near to you" (Jas 4:8). Read the passage again. Speak to the Father, or to the Son, in the Holy Spirit. Reclaim your identity as a beloved, welcomed, and cherished member of the Holy Trinity by your adoption into the Son. Be honest and open; be not afraid.

Contemplatio: Read the passage a third time. This time receive from God's Holy Spirit. Spend a little while abiding in God and letting God abide in you. Remain in him for a few minutes right here and right now.

SUGGESTIONS FOR JOURNALING

1. How have I experienced the love of the Father and the Son for me?
2. Have I remained in that love? What has caused me to wander from that love?
3. Where do I hear the voices of the world, the flesh, or the Devil seeking to deceive me by denying that I am beloved?
4. I felt the Spirit of God present within me when …
5. What helps me to remain in God's love is …
6. On the ninth day of Christmas, my True Love gave to me …

After you've journaled, close with a brief moment of gratitude and thanksgiving for today's prayer experience. Join with the Son and pray an Our Father in the Spirit of your adopted sonship.

January 3 — Saturday
Saturday Before Epiphany

THE HOLY NAME OF JESUS

Mary and Joseph were both instructed by angels to name their child "Jesus" (Lk 1:31; Mt 1:21). It was pronounced Y'shua in his native Aramaic and ΙΗΣΟΥΣ (Ye-sous) in the Greek language of the New Testament. This is "the name that is above every name, that at the name of Jesus every knee should bend, of those in heaven and on earth and under the earth" (Phil 2:9b–10). St. Bernardine of Siena preached on the Holy Name of Jesus using the monogram IHS (transliterated from the first three letters of Jesus' name in Greek) and added the Name of Jesus to the Hail Mary. This feast was added to the universal calendar in 1721, dropped in the reform after Vatican II, and re-added by Pope St. John Paul II.

REVIEW

Preparation: *Come, Holy Spirit, enlighten the eyes of my heart.* Call to mind God's loving care for you and spend the first minute of your prayer just resting in the free, unearned gift of loving and being loved. Let gratitude rise in your heart.

Glance through the past week, starting with Christmas Day. What grace and blessings have you received during the Christmas octave? Here are some questions to help you:

1. Where did I notice God, and what was he doing or saying?
2. How did I respond to what God was doing?
3. I felt God's love most strongly when …
4. I found myself struggling with …
5. I'm grateful for …
6. My strongest sense, image, moment, or experience of God's loving presence so far has been …
7. On the tenth day of Christmas, my True Love gave to me …

Conclude by conversing with God about your week. **Acknowledge** what you have been experiencing. **Relate** it to him. **Receive** what he wants to give you. **Respond** to him. Then savor that image of God's loving presence and rest there for a minute or two. Close with an Our Father.

Week Six

Announcement of Easter and the Movable Feasts for the Year of Our Lord 2026

The following text is traditionally read or chanted after the Gospel of Epiphany. It reminds us of the days when you couldn't just Google the date of Easter. It also reminds us that the mystery of God's love for us is not exhausted at Christmas. We are being invited to "stay tuned" for coming feast days:

> Know, dear brethren, (brothers and sisters), that, as we have rejoiced at the Nativity of our Lord Jesus Christ, so by leave of God's mercy we announce to you also the joy of his Resurrection, who is our Savior.
>
> On the eighteenth day of February will fall Ash Wednesday, and the beginning of the fast of the most sacred Lenten season.
>
> On the fifth of April you will celebrate with joy Easter Day, the Paschal feast of our Lord Jesus Christ.
>
> On the fourteenth day of May will be the Ascension of our Lord Jesus Christ. (Or the seventeenth day of May where the Ascension is transferred to Sunday.)
>
> On the twenty-fourth day of May, the feast of Pentecost.
>
> On the seventh of June, the feast of the Most Holy Body and Blood of Christ.
>
> On the twenty-ninth day of November, the First Sunday of the Advent of our Lord Jesus Christ, to whom is honor and glory for ever and ever. Amen.

We haven't even finished our Christmas journey and already we are being reminded of the date of next year's Advent. There is something very comforting in these words. The Church doesn't expect us to get everything right this year. We have another year in which to pray, fast, give alms, and grow closer to Jesus. If we keep putting one foot in front of another, we will make amazing progress one step at a time.

Grace of the Week: This week we celebrate the feast of the Epiphany twice, once as observed on Sunday and again on its proper day, January 6. Between these days are readings are all taken from the Book of Psalms. Ask God for the grace to welcome Jesus into your home and to follow him more faithfully into the new year.

January 4 — Sunday
Epiphany, Observed

The *Epiphany* is the manifestation of Jesus as Messiah of Israel, Son of God and Savior of the world. The great feast of Epiphany celebrates the adoration of Jesus by the wise men *(magi)* from the East, together with his baptism in the Jordan and the wedding feast at Cana in Galilee. In the magi, representatives of the neighboring pagan religions, the Gospel sees the first-fruits of the nations, who welcome the good news of salvation through the Incarnation. The magi's coming to Jerusalem in order to pay homage to the king of the Jews shows that they seek in Israel, in the messianic light of the star of David, the one who will be king of the nations. Their coming means that pagans can discover Jesus and worship him as Son of God and Savior of the world only by turning toward the Jews and receiving from them the messianic promise as contained in the Old Testament. The Epiphany shows that "the full number of the nations" now takes its "place in the family of the patriarchs," and acquires *Israelitica dignitas* (is made "worthy of the heritage of Israel"). (*Catechism of the Catholic Church*, 528)

Preparation: *Come, Holy Spirit, enlighten the eyes of my heart.* Be present to the God who is always present to you. Call to mind his loving care for you and spend the first minute of your prayer just resting in the free, unearned gift of loving and being loved. Let gratitude rise in your heart.

Set the Scene: Ask God for the grace to welcome Jesus into your home and to follow him more faithfully into the new year. Read through this passage slowly and prayerfully. Spend some time really setting the scene. What is the city like? What do the Magi look like? Picture the camels threading their way through the streets of Jerusalem, then Bethlehem. What does the house look like where the mother and child are?

MATTHEW 2:1–12 (LECTIONARY)
When Jesus was born in Bethlehem of Judea,
in the days of King Herod,
behold, magi from the east arrived in Jerusalem, saying,
"Where is the newborn king of the Jews?
We saw his star at its rising
and have come to do him homage."
When King Herod heard this,
he was greatly troubled,
and all Jerusalem with him.
Assembling all the chief priests and the scribes of the people,
he inquired of them where the Christ was to be born.
They said to him, "In Bethlehem of Judea,
for thus it has been written through the prophet:
And you, Bethlehem, land of Judah,
are by no means least among the rulers of Judah;
since from you shall come a ruler,
who is to shepherd my people Israel."
Then Herod called the magi secretly
and ascertained from them the time of the star's appearance.
He sent them to Bethlehem and said,
"Go and search diligently for the child.
When you have found him, bring me word,
that I too may go and do him homage."
After their audience with the king they set out.
And behold, the star that they had seen at its rising preceded them,
until it came and stopped over the place where the child was.
They were overjoyed at seeing the star,
and on entering the house
they saw the child with Mary his mother.
They prostrated themselves and did him homage.
Then they opened their treasures

and offered him gifts of gold, frankincense, and myrrh.
And having been warned in a dream not to return to Herod,
they departed for their country by another way.

Action! The Magi have made quite the pilgrimage. What was it like? Did they experience frustration? How did they encourage each other? What goes through their minds and hearts as they finally arrive? They find the child with his mother. Picture the relationship between mother and child. Read the passage a second time and let the scene unfold in your imagination.

Acknowledge: You, too, have been on a pilgrimage. What thoughts, feelings, and desires are rising in your heart?

Relate: Share your thoughts and feelings with Mary, the Mother of God. How does she respond to you?

Receive: Read the passage a third time. What does the mother want to tell you about her son? What does she want to tell you about yourself? What is in Mary's heart for you?

Respond: You have a gift to give. Open your treasures and respond by giving the Christ Child your gift.

SUGGESTIONS FOR JOURNALING
1. This time I was most drawn to …
2. I was particularly moved by …
3. The gift I want to give Jesus is …
4. I have been encouraged on this journey by …
5. Who have I encouraged on their pilgrimage of faith?
6. On the eleventh day of Christmas my True Love gave to me …

After you've journaled, close by spending a minute thanking God for your prayer experience today. Then pray a Hail Mary.

+

Bless your home today, or plan ahead for a blessing party on Tuesday. Instructions follow on the next page.

Blessing of the Home and Household on Epiphany

The custom of blessing homes while recalling the visit of the Magi is celebrated in many Old World countries. The C, M, and B of the inscription refer to the traditional names of the three Wise Men: Caspar, Melchior, and Balthasar. The numbers are the date of the current year. The family gathers. Candles are lit. It is most appropriate to gather around the Advent wreath, in which the purple candles have been replaced with white, but any white, non-scented candles may be lit.

The leader (preferably the father or eldest resident) begins by saying:

Peace be with this house and with all who live here. Blessed be the name of the Lord!

During these days of the Christmas season, we keep this feast of Epiphany, celebrating the manifestation of Christ to the Magi. Today, Christ is manifest to us! Today, this home is a holy place.

Let us pray:

> Father, we give you special thanks on this festival of the Epiphany, for leading the Magi from afar to the home of Christ, who has given light and hope to all peoples.
>
> By the power of the Holy Spirit, may his presence be renewed in our home.
>
> Make our home a place of human wholeness and divine holiness: a place of joy and laughter, a place of forgiveness and peace, a place of prayer, service, and discipleship.

The leader takes the blessed chalk and marks the lintel (the doorframe above the door) on the inside of the main entrance to the house as follows:

20 + C + M + B + 26
(insert the last two digits of the current year)

The prayer below is said during the marking by another family member, such as the other parent or a child:

> Loving God, as we mark this lintel, send the angel of mercy to guard our home and repel all powers of darkness. Fill those of us living here with a love for each other and warm us with the fullness of your presence and love.

After the lintel has been marked, the leader finishes by saying:

> Lord our God, you revealed your only-begotten Son to every nation by the guidance of a star.
> Bless now this household with health, goodness of heart, gentleness, and the keeping of your law of love.
> May all who visit this dwelling find here:
> the tender loving care of Mary, the God-bearer, the prayerful protection of Saint Joseph, the faithful perseverance of the magi, and the humble peace of the Christ Child,
> the light of the nations, and thus praise you for all eternity in the unity of the Holy Spirit and the Church, now and forever.

All respond: Amen.

All join hands and pray together the Our Father. The leader then invites all to share a sign of peace.

Other doors may be marked by family members, especially children marking the doors of their own bedrooms. If possible, the family may continue the celebration by sharing a special meal together.

January 5 — Monday
Monday After Epiphany

ST. JOHN NEUMANN, BISHOP (USA), MEMORIAL

Born in 1811 in Bohemia (the western half of the present-day Czech Republic), John felt a desire to be an American missionary. He was ordained in New York in 1834. He worked to establish parishes and schools in Maryland, Virginia, and Ohio. He became bishop of Philadelphia at the age of forty-one and organized the parochial school system that helped define the Catholic experience in the United States.

Preparation: *Come, Holy Spirit, enlighten the eyes of my heart.* Be present to the God who is always present to you. Call to mind his loving care for you and spend the first minute of your prayer just resting in the free, unearned gift of loving and being loved. Let gratitude rise in your heart.

Lectio: Ask God for the grace to welcome Jesus into your home and to follow him more faithfully into the new year. Today's psalm was originally intended as a song for the coronation of a king. It was common in the ancient world to see kings as endowed with divine power. Some pagan kings even had themselves declared gods and demanded worship from their people. Here, we see this psalm as a prophecy that God will set up his son Jesus Christ as the King of Kings and lord of all peoples. He alone is worthy of worship because he is true God and true man. Read the passage slowly and prayerfully.

PSALM 2:7BC–8, 10–12A (LECTIONARY)

*The L*ORD *said to me, "you are my Son;*
this day I have begotten you.
Ask of me and I will give you
the nations for an inheritance
and the ends of the earth for your possession."

And now, O kings, give heed;

> *take warning, you rulers of the earth.*
> *Serve the* LORD *with fear, and rejoice before him;*
> *with trembling rejoice.*

Meditatio: The kings of this world punish those who fail to submit to them. Jesus does not compel anyone to worship him. However, at the end of time, he will be revealed as the true King. Those who have served him will receive rewards in his eternal kingdom, and those who have rejected him will find themselves cast out of his kingdom. Those who temporarily rule on earth would do well to take warning and pay heed. What does it mean that the nations are his inheritance? How can one both "serve the Lord with fear" and "rejoice before him"?

Oratio: Read the passage a second time. The meek will inherit the earth (see Mt 5:5), and these words especially apply to Jesus (Mt 11:29). How does it feel that, in the end, the humble babe born in Bethlehem will be the true king of the universe? He is the King of Hearts who loves his subjects enough to die for them. He is also with you right now and he cares about what is on your heart. Speak to him with confidence and candor. How does he receive what is on your heart?

Contemplatio: Read the passage a third time. This time receive from Jesus what he desires to communicate to you. He cares about every subject, no matter how small or meek they might feel. Spend some time abiding with Jesus and letting him abide with you.

SUGGESTIONS FOR JOURNALING
1. The word or phrase that most spoke to me was ...
2. I received a new insight or understanding that ...
3. Jesus wanted to remind me ...
4. I found peace and joy when ...
5. On the twelfth day of Christmas, my True Love gave to me ...

Monday After Epiphany **187**

After you've journaled, close with a brief moment of gratitude and thanksgiving for today's prayer experience. Then pray an Our Father with fear and rejoicing.

January 6 — Tuesday
The Epiphany of the Lord (Traditional)

The name *Epiphany* means "manifestation." Through the arrival of the Wise Men (Magi) from the East, Jesus is manifest as not only the King of the Jews, but as the Savior of all peoples and a light for all the nations. The Eastern Churches refer to this day as "Little Christmas" or "Theophany." Many cultures have special traditions associated with this feast, including parades, special foods, and gift-giving. In the United States, the liturgical celebration of the Epiphany is always transferred to the Sunday between January 2 and January 8. However, there's no reason we cannot celebrate this feast also on its proper day.

Preparation: *Come, Holy Spirit, enlighten the eyes of my heart.* Be present to the God who is always present to you. Call to mind his loving care for you and spend the first minute of your prayer just resting in the free, unearned gift of loving and being loved. Let gratitude rise in your heart.

Lectio: Ask God for the grace to welcome Jesus into your home and to follow him more faithfully into the new year. This passage is taken from the feast day that we celebrated on Sunday. The Jews were God's Chosen People. Their special mission and purpose began when God called Abraham and made a covenant with him. Saint Paul has come to realize that the Jews were chosen precisely to prepare for the coming of Jesus Christ, God's only-begotten Son, who is meant for all the world. Read the passage slowly and prayerfully.

EPHESIANS 3:2–3A, 5–6 (LECTIONARY)
Brothers and sisters:
You have heard of the stewardship of God's grace
that was given to me for your benefit,
namely, that the mystery was made known to me by revelation.

*It was not made known to people in other generations
as it has now been revealed
to his holy apostles and prophets by the Spirit:
that the Gentiles are coheirs, members of the same body,
and copartners in the promise in Christ Jesus through the
    gospel.*

Meditatio: Jews saw the world through the great divisions of light and darkness, life and death, clean and unclean, Jew and Gentile. They would be shocked to hear that unclean Gentiles are now "members of the same body" as Jews. But for Saint Paul, the coming of Jesus changes everything. We all need him as a Savior, and we are all invited through baptism to become incorporated (literally, "combined in one body") into Jesus Christ. What does it mean that Christians are so united with Christ that they have become parts of his body?

Oratio: Read the passage a second time. You are now a "copartner in the promise in Christ Jesus through the gospel." How does this revelation make you feel? Speak to God whatever is on your heart and mind today. How does he receive your thoughts, feelings, and desires?

Contemplatio: Read the passage a third time. Is there something Jesus wants you to know? Receive from Jesus whatever he has for you. Then rest in communion with him, a communion so deep that it is like you are "one body" with Jesus Christ.

SUGGESTIONS FOR JOURNALING
1. The word or phrase that most spoke to me was …
2. I received a new insight or understanding that …
3. Jesus wanted to remind me …
4. I have a hard time accepting that …
5. I found peace and joy when …

190 *January 6 — Tuesday*

After you've journaled, close with a brief moment of gratitude and thanksgiving for today's prayer experience. Then pray an Our Father.

January 7 — Wednesday
Wednesday After Epiphany

ST. ANDRÉ BESSETTE (CANADA)

Born August 9, 1845, to a French-Canadian couple, he was the eighth of twelve children. By the time he was twelve, both his parents had died, leaving him an orphan. He developed a deep devotion to Saint Joseph. At the age of twenty-five, he applied to the Congregation of the Holy Cross. Weak health extended his novitiate, but he was finally accepted and given the job of doorkeeper at Notre Dame College in Montreal. He would joke, "When I joined this community, the superiors showed me the door, and I remained forty years." The sick came to be prayed for and many were healed. When an epidemic broke out in a nearby hospital, he volunteered to nurse the sick, and not a single person died. His healing powers became famous, though he always gave credit to Saint Joseph. He died on January 6, 1937, and was buried in the magnificent oratory on Mont Royal that was the fruit of his labors and faith. He is celebrated on January 6 in the United States and on January 7 in his home country.

Preparation: *Come, Holy Spirit, enlighten the eyes of my heart.* Be present to the God who is always present to you. Call to mind his loving care for you and spend the first minute of your prayer just resting in the free, unearned gift of loving and being loved. Let gratitude rise in your heart.

Lectio: Ask God for the grace to welcome Jesus into your home and to follow him more faithfully into the new year. The notes for the *New American Bible* explain today's passages, saying, "A royal Psalm in which the Israelite king, as the representative of God, is the instrument of divine justice and blessing for the whole world." The extravagant, superlative language would be typical of royal courts in the ancient Near East. Is it too much to hope for a king who rules with justice and peace and cares for the poor? Not if this king is the Son of God! Picture Jesus seated on the lap of his mother as the Magi do him homage and present him with gifts. Read the passage slowly and prayerfully.

PSALM 72:1–2, 7–8, 10–11, 12–13 (LECTIONARY)

O God, with your judgment endow the king,
and with your justice, the king's son;
He shall govern your people with justice
and your afflicted ones with judgment.

Justice shall flower in his days,
and profound peace, till the moon be no more.
May he rule from sea to sea,
and from the River to the ends of the earth.

The kings of Tarshish and the Isles shall offer gifts;
the kings of Arabia and Seba shall bring tribute.
All kings shall pay him homage,
all nations shall serve him.

For he shall rescue the poor when he cries out,
and the afflicted when he has no one to help him.
He shall have pity for the lowly and the poor;
the lives of the poor he shall save.

Meditatio: Tarshish and the islands sit to the far west of Israel; Sheba and Seba to the distant southeast. Even these distant kingdoms have not only heard of the king, but also come to pay tribute to him. In what ways does the kingdom of Jesus Christ extend "to the ends of the earth"? How does he rescue the poor when they cry out? Meditate on how this psalm has come true in ways the psalmist could not have imagined.

Oratio: Read the passage a second time. What do you have to offer God? What gifts can you lay before the king? Search the treasury of your heart for the thing Jesus most wants to receive from you. Picture yourself entering the house as the fourth Wise Man, or perhaps as one of the poor that Jesus desires to save. Speak to him from your heart.

Contemplatio: Read the passage a third time. What does Jesus want to give you: peace, justice, rescue, pity? He is a generous king and has gifts in abundance for you. Receive whatever is in the king's heart for you. Rejoice and praise him for his goodness. Perhaps it is your friendship that he most desires. Rejoice in his humble presence with you for a few minutes before moving on.

SUGGESTIONS FOR JOURNALING
1. The phrase from the psalm that most spoke to me was …
2. When I see Jesus as a king, I think of …
3. I wanted to give Jesus …
4. Jesus wanted to give me …
5. I ended prayer with a stronger or deeper sense of …

January 7 — Wednesday

After you've journaled, close with a brief conversation thanking the King for your prayer time today. Then pray an Our Father.

January 8 — Thursday
Thursday After Epiphany

Preparation: *Come, Holy Spirit, enlighten the eyes of my heart.* Be present to the God who is always present to you. Call to mind his loving care for you and spend the first minute of your prayer just resting in the free, unearned gift of loving and being loved. Let gratitude rise in your heart.

Lectio: Ask God for the grace to welcome Jesus into your home and to follow him more faithfully into the new year. Yesterday we meditated on God's gift of a king that would rule over all nations. However, we all experience oppression to some extent. The poor suffer oppression the most. How does God want to respond to their experiences? Read the passage slowly and prayerfully.

PSALM 72:1–2, 14 AND 15BC, 17 (LECTIONARY)
O God, with your judgment endow the king,
and with your justice, the king's son;
He shall govern your people with justice
and your afflicted ones with judgment.

From fraud and violence he shall redeem them,
and precious shall their blood be in his sight.
May they be prayed for continually;
day by day shall they bless him.

May his name be blessed forever;
as long as the sun his name shall remain.
In him shall all the tribes of the earth be blessed;
all the nations shall proclaim his happiness.

Meditatio: When Cain kills Abel, God says to Cain, "What have you done? Your brother's blood cries out to me from the ground" (Gn 4:9). God intends to settle the score with those who subject others to fraud and violence. He speaks of prayer being offered continually for them, and those who have suffered respond with blessings. Have you suffered injustice? Does it look differently if your blood is precious to God? Have you been guilty of injustice toward others?

Oratio: Read the passage a second time. Talk to God about the things that were stirred up in you by the meditation. He is a just and merciful God. He desires to save you. What do you want to say to him?

Contemplatio: Read the passage a third time. What is in Jesus' heart for you? Receive whatever your king has to give you. Bless him and proclaim his happiness, then remain with him for a little while.

SUGGESTIONS FOR JOURNALING
1. The injustice that most troubles me is …
2. The phrase from the psalm that most spoke to me was …
3. Jesus wanted me to know …
4. I feel moved to action …

After you've journaled, close with a brief conversation thanking the King for your prayer time today. Then pray an Our Father.

January 9 — Friday
Friday After Epiphany

Preparation: *Come, Holy Spirit, enlighten the eyes of my heart.* Be present to the God who is always present to you. Call to mind his loving care for you and spend the first minute of your prayer just resting in the free, unearned gift of loving and being loved. Let gratitude rise in your heart.

Lectio: Ask God for the grace to welcome Jesus into your home and to follow him more faithfully into the new year. Bible passages can be understood in four senses. First, they can be understood in reference to historic realities. The rebuilding of Jerusalem is about the return from exile and the literal project that took place to return the ruined city to good order. Second, they can be understood in terms of final realities, that is, the plan of God to restore all things when he creates the new heavens and the new earth. Third, they can refer to the moral life, that is, restoring our own souls to good order. Finally, they can refer to Jesus Christ. Look for what most speaks to you as you read the passage slowly and prayerfully.

PSALM 147
I
Hallelujah!

How good to sing praise to our God;
  how pleasant to give fitting praise.
The L*ord* *rebuilds Jerusalem,*
  and gathers the dispersed of Israel,
Healing the brokenhearted,
  and binding up their wounds.
He numbers the stars,
  and gives to all of them their names.
Great is our Lord, vast in power,
  with wisdom beyond measure.
The L*ord* *gives aid to the poor,*
  but casts the wicked to the ground.

II
Sing to the L*ord* *with thanksgiving;*
  with the lyre make music to our God,
Who covers the heavens with clouds,
  provides rain for the earth,
  makes grass sprout on the mountains,
Who gives animals their food
  and young ravens what they cry for.
He takes no delight in the strength of horses,
  no pleasure in the runner's stride.
Rather the L*ord* *takes pleasure in those who fear him,*
  those who put their hope in his mercy.

III
Glorify the L*ord**, Jerusalem;*
  Zion, offer praise to your God,
For he has strengthened the bars of your gates,
  blessed your children within you.
He brings peace to your borders,
  and satisfies you with finest wheat.
He sends his command to earth;
  his word runs swiftly!
Thus he makes the snow like wool,
  and spreads the frost like ash;
He disperses hail like crumbs.
  Who can withstand his cold?
Yet when again he issues his command, it melts them;
  he raises his winds and the waters flow.
He proclaims his word to Jacob,
  his statutes and laws to Israel.
He has not done this for any other nation;
  of such laws they know nothing.
Hallelujah!

Meditatio: You will notice similar themes here to many other passages of Scripture that we have meditated on. When have you experienced God's rebuilding, restoring, or putting to good order in your life?

***Oratio*:** Read the passage a second time. It shares a beautiful vision of harmony, hope, and peace — which is at odds with our usual experiences in the world today. What longings does this passage stir up in your heart? Notice your desires, then share them openly and honestly with God.

***Contemplatio*:** This third time, just read the part of the passage that most speaks to you. How does God want to respond to the desires of your heart? He who feeds and cares for the animals surely knows what will delight and satisfy you. Do you have confidence in his loving care for you? Remain with him a while before moving on.

SUGGESTIONS FOR JOURNALING

1. The phrase from the psalm that most spoke to me was ...
2. I found myself longing for...
3. Jesus wanted me to know...
4. I found hope in...

After you've journaled, close with a brief conversation thanking God for spending time with you today. Then pray an Our Father.

January 10 — Saturday
Saturday After Epiphany

REVIEW

Preparation: *Come, Holy Spirit, enlighten the eyes of my heart.* Call to mind God's loving care for you this past week and spend the first minute of your prayer just resting in the free, unearned gift of loving and being loved. Let gratitude rise in your heart.

Let's take some time to review our prayer this week. Note that you can also repeat a prayer time or do it for the first time if you missed a day or two. But first, flip back through your past week's journal entries. As you do, notice what emerged in the conversation. Here are some questions to help you:

1. Where did I notice God, and what was he doing or saying?
2. How did I respond to what God was doing?
3. I felt most like a child of God when …
4. I struggle to see myself as a child of God when (or because) …
5. I'm grateful for …
6. This past week, my strongest sense, image, moment, or experience of God's loving presence was …
7. Following God more faithfully in the new year will look like…

Conclude by conversing with God about your week. **Acknowledge** what you have been experiencing. **Relate** it to him. **Receive** what he wants to give you. **Respond** to him. Then savor that image of God's loving presence and rest there for a minute or two. Close with an Our Father.

Week Seven

Keep the Christmas Light Burning Brightly

Officially, the Catholic celebration of Christmas ends on the feast of the Baptism of the Lord (usually a Sunday, except when Epiphany is transferred forward to January 7 or 8). However, there seems to have been a popular tradition of stretching Christmas out as long as possible. We do the same thing, I suppose, by moving the beginning of the "Christmas Season" earlier and earlier. Our ancestors, on the other hand, started on Christmas Day and didn't end until February 2. Does that date sound familiar? Most people recognize that date as the strange, secular holiday Groundhog Day. In the Christian calendar, this date is the feast of the Presentation, also known by the old English name of *Candlemas*.

As a newly ordained priest, I was getting ready for daily Mass on February 2. I opened the Roman Missal to the feast of the Presentation and was expecting to find just the normal extra prayers. Instead, there was a long instruction about how to begin outside of church with the blessing of candles and process into church carrying lit candles. I'd never experienced this before. Later, when Candlemas fell on a Sunday, I found that many priests didn't quite know what to do with this day. This feast clearly used to be a big deal and is almost forgotten now.

Why would our ancestors have made a big deal out of this day? Lit candles are a symbol of faith. Baptized infants and adults are given a lit candle and told to "keep the flame of faith alive in your heart." They harken back to the candles on the Advent wreath that lit up our home as the world grew darker. They also foreshadow the candlelight procession of the Easter Vigil. Remember how we spend forty days in Lenten fasting, followed by fifty days of Easter feasting? So, celebrating Candlemas as the end of Christmas gives us up to twenty-eight days of Advent preparation followed by forty days of Christmas celebration.

The celebration of Christmas makes more sense when it ends on Candlemas. We need the lights and cheer especially during the dreary days of January. Your Advent waiting is rewarded when you take the time to savor a longer Christmas. It's no wonder that the English in Tudor times left their holly and ivy and other greenery up until Candlemas. Even though the liturgical season of Christmas will be over, your own personal celebration can continue. I encourage you to keep your Advent wreath and Nativity scene up in the spirit of the old English tradition (and even your Christmas tree, as long as it is not a crispy fire hazard). Keep praying and keep savoring the light of Christ shining from the manger scene. God has more to give. Let us keep our hearts open to receive.

Grace of the Week: This week we will return to Ordinary Time, both in the liturgical season and in our lives. Our readings are drawn from the daily Mass readings. We have seen God present in the shining moments of Christmas. His ordinary presence may be less bright now, but keep your eyes open and you will find him no less present. Ask God for the grace to see your Savior in a new light, and to hear his voice calling you to follow him.

January 11 — Sunday
Baptism of the Lord

The Baptism of the Lord marks a transition from Jesus' hidden life in Nazareth to his public ministry of teaching and healing that will ultimately culminate in his death on the cross:

> The baptism of Jesus is on his part the acceptance and inauguration of his mission as God's suffering Servant. He allows himself to be numbered among sinners; he is already "the Lamb of God, who takes away the son of the world." Already he is anticipating the "baptism" of his bloody death. Already he is coming to "fulfill all righteousness," that is, he is submitting himself entirely to his Father's will: out of love he consents to this baptism of death for the remission of our sins. The Father's voice responds to the Son's acceptance, proclaiming his entire delight in his Son. The Spirit whom Jesus possessed in fullness from his conception comes to "rest on him." Jesus will be the source of the Spirit for all mankind. At his baptism "the heavens were opened" — the heavens that Adam's sin had closed — and the waters were sanctified by the descent of Jesus and the Spirit, a prelude to the new creation. (CCC 536)

Preparation: *Come, Holy Spirit, enlighten the eyes of my heart.* Be present to the God who is always present to you. Call to mind his loving care for you and spend the first minute of your prayer just resting in the free, unearned gift of loving and being loved. Let gratitude rise in your heart.

Set the Scene: Ask God for the grace that the Christmas light might continue to enlighten dark places in your heart. John the Baptist has been preaching in the wilderness of Judea, telling the people: "Repent, for the kingdom of heaven is at hand" (Mt 3:2). He wears a rough garment of camel's hair and feeds on locusts and wild honey. Picture the people coming out into the wilderness from the city of Jerusalem and the region of Judea, listening to John preaching, confessing their sins, and being baptized in the Jordan River. Among the throng of sinners stands the one mightier than John, whose sandals he is not worthy to carry (see Mt 3:11). Read the passage and use your imagination to set the scene.

MATTHEW 3:13–17 (LECTIONARY)

Jesus came from Galilee to John at the Jordan
to be baptized by him.
John tried to prevent him, saying,
"I need to be baptized by you,
and yet you are coming to me?"
Jesus said to him in reply,
"Allow it now, for thus it is fitting for us
to fulfill all righteousness."
Then he allowed him.
After Jesus was baptized,
he came up from the water and behold,
the heavens were opened for him,
and he saw the Spirit of God descending like a dove
and coming upon him.
And a voice came from the heavens, saying,
"This is my beloved Son, with whom I am well pleased."

Action! The baptism that John offers is a visible sign of new life. People confess their sins and resolve to do better. They drown their old life in the waters of the river and come out the other side a new person, or at least a person committed to a better way of life. Pharisees and Sadducees are coming for baptism, but with no desire to start a new life because they think they are already righteous (see Mt 3:7–10). Among all the sinners stands Jesus himself, the sinless one. Surely, Jesus is the one man who doesn't need to be baptized. John pauses as he seems to notice this incongruity. Why does Jesus choose to join the sinners? Why does he receive baptism? Ponder these questions as you play through the scene in your imagination.

Acknowledge: Read the passage a second time. This time, picture yourself somewhere in the scene. Do you line up for baptism with all the sinners? Are you hanging back, skeptical or distant or afraid? Notice the thoughts and feelings inside of you. Welcome them without judging them.

Relate: Jesus is with you, perhaps drying off in the hot sun. Sit with Jesus by the Jordan River. Share with him what is on your heart.

Receive: How does Jesus respond to what you have shared with him? Listen to Jesus' heart. Why was he baptized, and what did it mean to him? Many of us were baptized when we were too young to remember it. But Jesus was there, and so was the Father and the Holy Spirit. Let them tell you about it. Be open to whatever God is offering — a word, thought, or feeling, a new understanding or insight. Read the passage a third time and see this moment, and yourself, through Jesus' eyes.

Respond: Continue the conversation for a little while. Then just rest in the love God has for you, the same love that the Father has for his only-begotten Son.

SUGGESTIONS FOR JOURNALING
1. The part that stood out to me from today's reading was …
2. My most prominent thought, feeling, or desire was …
3. Jesus wanted to show me or teach me …
4. I ended prayer wanting …
5. I now see my own baptism in a new way …

212 *January 11 — Sunday*

After you've journaled, close with a brief conversation giving thanks to God, Father, Son, and Spirit for your prayer experience. Then pray an Our Father.

January 12 – Monday
Monday of the First Week in Ordinary Time

Preparation: *Come, Holy Spirit, enlighten the eyes of my heart.* Be present to the God who is always present to you. Call to mind his loving care for you and spend the first minute of your prayer just resting in the free, unearned gift of loving and being loved. Let gratitude rise in your heart.

Set the Scene: Ask God for the grace that the Christmas light might continue to enlighten dark places in your heart. Read the passage to set the scene. The ancient world did not understand genetics as we do today. They saw childbearing as a matter of soil and seed (the word *semen* means "seed" in Latin). The man was the sower and the woman was the garden; the man planted his seed in the soil of a woman's womb and then waited to see what would grow. When nothing grew, year after year, the woman would have been seen, and considered herself to be, barren soil.

1 SAMUEL 1:1–8
*There was a certain man from Ramathaim, a Zuphite from the hill country of Ephraim. His name was Elkanah, the son of Jeroham, son of Elihu, son of Tohu, son of Zuph, an Ephraimite. He had two wives, one named Hannah, the other Peninnah; Peninnah had children, but Hannah had no children. Each year this man went up from his city to worship and offer sacrifice to the L*ord *of hosts at Shiloh, where the two sons of Eli, Hophni and Phinehas, were ministering as priests of the L*ord*. When the day came for Elkanah to offer sacrifice, he used to give portions to his wife Peninnah and to all her sons and daughters, but he would give a double portion to Hannah because he loved her, though the L*ord *had closed her womb. Her rival, to upset her, would torment her constantly, since the L*ord *had closed her womb. Year after year, when she went up*

> to the house of the Lord, Peninnah would provoke her, and Hannah would weep and refuse to eat. Elkanah, her husband, would say to her: "Hannah, why are you weeping? Why are you not eating? Why are you so miserable? Am I not better for you than ten sons?"

Action! Hannah's husband loves her and doesn't hold her infertility against her. But she sees herself as a big failure, and the other wife treats her that way too. Her grief seems to always ruin the family pilgrimage. The narrator blames God for not blessing her with children. What is going on in the hearts of the characters in today's reading?

Acknowledge: Have you felt like a failure? Have you ever felt that God let you down? When have you felt so burdened by grief that you couldn't eat? Do you have a rival who torments you constantly? Perhaps think back to your younger years. Notice what is going on in your heart as you read this passage again.

Relate: God is with you. Speak to him about what is going on in your heart. You can even yell at him if you need to.

Receive: How does God respond to the things you are sharing? Hannah is not open to her husband's kindness, but you can be open to whatever God is offering you: a word, thought, a feeling, or a new perspective. Read the passage a third time in a mode of receiving.

Respond: Continue the conversation for a little while. Then just rest in the love God has for you, the same love that Jesus experienced from his Father at his baptism.

SUGGESTIONS FOR JOURNALING
1. I feel like a failure when ...
2. I have been burdened by ...
3. I sensed God was with me and wanted me to know ...
4. My prayer today gave me a new insight into how I should think, respond, or act ...

5. I am comforted by the realization that …

After you've journaled, close with a brief conversation with God giving thanks for your prayer experience. Then pray the Our Father.

January 13 — Tuesday
Tuesday of the First Week in Ordinary Time

Preparation: *Come, Holy Spirit, enlighten the eyes of my heart.* Be present to the God who is always present to you. Call to mind his loving care for you and spend the first minute of your prayer just resting in the free, unearned gift of loving and being loved. Let gratitude rise in your heart.

Set the Scene: Ask God for the grace that the Christmas light might continue to enlighten dark places in your heart. Read the passage slowly and prayerfully. Picture the scene in your mind. In the ancient world, people generally prayed out loud to make sure that God heard them. The shrine at Shiloh would not have been a quiet place when it was full of people. Hannah, however, is so emotional that she can't form audible words. This leads the priest to presume that she is a babbling drunk. Could it get any worse for her?

1 SAMUEL 1:9–20

> Hannah rose after one such meal at Shiloh, and presented herself before the Lord; at the time Eli the priest was sitting on a chair near the doorpost of the Lord's temple. In her bitterness she prayed to the Lord, weeping freely, and made this vow: "O Lord of hosts, if you look with pity on the hardship of your servant, if you remember me and do not forget me, if you give your handmaid a male child, I will give him to the Lord all the days of his life. No razor shall ever touch his head." As she continued praying before the Lord, Eli watched her mouth, for Hannah was praying silently; though her lips were moving, her voice could not be heard. Eli, thinking she was drunk, said to her, "How long will you make a drunken spectacle of yourself? Sober up from your wine!" "No, my lord!" Hannah answered. "I am an unhappy woman. I have had neither wine nor li-

quor; I was only pouring out my heart to the LORD. *Do not think your servant a worthless woman; my prayer has been prompted by my deep sorrow and misery." Eli said, "Go in peace, and may the God of Israel grant you what you have requested." She replied, "Let your servant find favor in your eyes," and left. She went to her quarters, ate and drank with her husband, and no longer appeared downhearted. Early the next morning they worshiped before the* LORD, *and then returned to their home in Ramah. When they returned Elkanah had intercourse with his wife Hannah, and the* LORD *remembered her.*

She conceived and, at the end of her pregnancy, bore a son whom she named Samuel. "Because I asked the LORD *for him."*

Action! Play the scene out in your mind. The comments of the priest Eli do not discourage her. Hannah has left her grief with the Lord and trusted him to take care of her problems. Picture her at prayer and again after the little blessing that Eli gives her. How does she feel?

Acknowledge: Read the passage again. What does this passage stir up in your heart — what thoughts, desires, hopes, fears?

Relate: Take your place on the ground at Shiloh and pour out your heart to God. Tell him honestly what is burdening you, as Hannah did.

Receive: How does God respond to the things you are sharing? Be open to receive whatever response you get: a word, thought, or feeling, or just the confidence that God will take it from here. Read the passage a third time.

Respond: Thank God for whatever he is giving you. Cherish his loving care for you and rest in it for a few minutes before moving on.

SUGGESTIONS FOR JOURNALING
1. What struck me most was …
2. I felt burdened by …

3. God lifted my burdens when …
4. God answered my prayers with …
5. I left prayer with a new insight, understanding, or confidence that …

After you've journaled, close with a brief conversation giving thanks to God for your prayer experience. Then pray one Our Father.

January 14 — Wednesday
Wednesday of the First Week in Ordinary Time

Preparation: *Come, Holy Spirit, enlighten the eyes of my heart.* Be present to the God who is always present to you. Call to mind his loving care for you and spend the first minute of your prayer just resting in the free, unearned gift of loving and being loved. Let gratitude rise in your heart.

Set the Scene: Ask God for the grace that the Christmas light might continue to enlighten dark places in your heart. Read the passage through. Once Samuel was weaned, Hannah returned to the Temple and presented him to the Lord, as she had promised (see 1 Sm 1:21–28). His family would see him on their yearly visit to the shrine, and God blessed Hannah with five more children (2:18–21). Samuel is raised in the Temple and takes care of Eli in his old age. Perhaps Samuel is now sleeping in the very spot where his mother once prayed for the gift of a child. Picture the scene.

1 SAMUEL 3:1–10, 19–20

During the time young Samuel was minister to the LORD under Eli, the word of the LORD was scarce and vision infrequent. One day Eli was asleep in his usual place. His eyes had lately grown so weak that he could not see. The lamp of God was not yet extinguished, and Samuel was sleeping in the temple of the LORD where the ark of God was. The LORD called to Samuel, who answered, "Here I am." He ran to Eli and said, "Here I am. You called me." "I did not call you," Eli answered. "Go back to sleep." So he went back to sleep. Again the LORD called Samuel, who rose and went to Eli. "Here I am," he said. "You called me." But he answered, "I did not call you, my son. Go back to sleep."

Samuel did not yet recognize the LORD, since the word

of the L*ord* *had not yet been revealed to him. The* L*ord* *called Samuel again, for the third time. Getting up and going to Eli, he said, "Here I am. You called me." Then Eli understood that the* L*ord* *was calling the youth. So he said to Samuel, "Go to sleep, and if you are called, reply, 'Speak,* L*ord,* *for your servant is listening.'" When Samuel went to sleep in his place, the* L*ord* *came and stood there, calling out as before: Samuel, Samuel! Samuel answered, "Speak, for your servant is listening."*

Samuel grew up, and the L*ord* *was with him, not permitting any word of his to go unfulfilled. Thus all Israel from Dan to Beer-sheba came to know that Samuel was a trustworthy prophet of the* L*ord.*

Action! Play the scene forward in your mind. How many of us would have stayed in bed the third time we thought Eli was calling us? Yet Samuel responds with the same eagerness and generosity each time he hears the call. What is going on in his heart?

Acknowledge: Read the passage again. Though Samuel was sleeping in the Temple, he never imagined that God himself would speak to him. Do you expect God to call you, or to respond to your prayers? Do you think yourself unworthy of a conversation with the Almighty? What is going on in your heart as you read this passage?

Relate: Share your heart with God, the same God who spoke to Samuel.

Receive: Now it is your turn to listen. Say, "Speak. For your servant is listening." Give God some silent time to respond to you. Read the passage again with the same patient persistence of Samuel.

Respond: Know that God can call you at any time, and can answer your prayers whenever he chooses. Don't expect God to stop talking just because you have finished your prayer. But for now, be grateful for whatever thought, word, desire, or new insight you might have received in this prayer time.

SUGGESTIONS FOR JOURNALING
1. My favorite part of today's prayer was …
2. I was not expecting …
3. God surprised me with …
4. I can most easily hear God when …
5. What makes it hard for me to listen to God's voice is …

After you've journaled, close with a brief conversation with God giving thanks for your prayer experience. Then pray the Our Father.

January 15 — Thursday
Thursday of the First Week in Ordinary Time

Preparation: *Come, Holy Spirit, enlighten the eyes of my heart.* Be present to the God who is always present to you. Call to mind his loving care for you and spend the first minute of your prayer just resting in the free, unearned gift of loving and being loved. Let gratitude rise in your heart.

Set the Scene: Ask God for the grace that the Christmas light might continue to enlighten dark places in your heart. Read the passage through once. Eli himself is a good priest, but he has raised wicked sons. God has prophesied evil against them in response to the evil they have done (see 1 Sm 2:34; 3:11–14). Now we see the prophecies come true.

1 SAMUEL 4:1–11

*At that time, the Philistines gathered for an attack on Israel. Israel went out to engage them in battle and camped at Ebenezer, while the Philistines camped at Aphek. The Philistines then drew up in battle formation against Israel. After a fierce struggle Israel was defeated by the Philistines, who killed about four thousand men on the battlefield. When the troops retired to the camp, the elders of Israel said, "Why has the L*ord *permitted us to be defeated today by the Philistines? Let us fetch the ark of the L*ord *from Shiloh that it may go into battle among us and save us from the grasp of our enemies."*

*So the people sent to Shiloh and brought from there the ark of the L*ord *of hosts, who is enthroned upon the cherubim. The two sons of Eli, Hophni and Phinehas, accompanied the ark of God. When the ark of the L*ord *arrived in the camp, all Israel shouted so loudly that the earth shook. The Philistines, hearing the uproar, asked, "What does this loud shouting in the camp of the Hebrews* mean?" On learning that the ark of the LORD had come into the camp, the Philistines were frightened, crying out, "Gods have come to their camp. Woe to us! This has never happened before. Woe to us! Who can deliver us from the power of these mighty gods? These are the gods who struck the Egyptians with various plagues in the desert. Take courage and act like soldiers, Philistines; otherwise you will become slaves to the Hebrews, as they were your slaves. Fight like soldiers!" The Philistines fought and Israel was defeated; everyone fled to their own tents. It was a disastrous defeat; Israel lost thirty thousand foot soldiers. The ark of God was captured, and Eli's two sons, Hophni and Phinehas, were dead.

Action! The ancient world thought that victory in battle came from their gods prevailing over the gods of their enemies. The people of Israel bring out the Ark of the Covenant like one might drop a trump card in a card game. This Ark destroyed the walls of Jericho and brought them safely to the promised land. It will certainly give them victory over the Philistines. However, those victories were won because the people were listening to God and following his instructions. The wickedness of their priests has now caused the people to stray; they are no longer obedient to God. Their strength has left them like Samson with a haircut (see Jgs 16:18–21).

Acknowledge: Read the passage again and pay attention to what is going on in your heart. Where have you felt the sting of defeat? When have you expected God to come to your rescue and, instead of answering your prayers, things got worse? Channel those feelings as you read the passage a second time.

Relate: Now speak to God whatever is in your heart; share your failures and disappointments and defeats with him.

Receive: Read the passage again. How does God respond to what you have shared with him? Is there some thought, feeling, or image? Or perhaps a kind of disturbing silence, like he hasn't heard? If you really don't hear anything from God, and you find yourself frustrated with the conversation, you can also tell him about that. Say something like, "God, when I poured out my heart to you, and I heard nothing in return, it made me feel ..."

Respond: Continue the conversation, or perhaps answer silence with silence. Know that God's response always comes from a place of love. If you hear nothing, it doesn't mean he is busy or distracted. It just means you need to keep looking and listening with your heart.

SUGGESTIONS FOR JOURNALING

1. Where have I felt the sting of failure or defeat?
2. When did God not seem to be answering my prayers?
3. What was one important lesson I learned through failure or defeat or the silence of God?
4. I was surprised by ...
5. A new insight I received was ...

After you've journaled, close with a brief conversation with God giving thanks for your prayer experience. Then pray an Our Father.

January 16 — Friday
Friday of the First Week in Ordinary Time

Preparation: *Come, Holy Spirit, enlighten the eyes of my heart.* Be present to the God who is always present to you. Call to mind his loving care for you and spend the first minute of your prayer just resting in the free, unearned gift of loving and being loved. Let gratitude rise in your heart.

Lectio: Ask God for the grace that the Christmas light might continue to enlighten dark places in your heart. Read the passage through, slowly and prayerfully. Up until this point, there has not been a king in Israel. The twelve tribes have been guided by the judges and the prophets. Sadly, Samuel's sons are no better than Eli's were. And the people want to be like the other nations.

1 SAMUEL 8:4–7, 10–22

Therefore all the elders of Israel assembled and went to Samuel at Ramah and said to him, "Now that you are old, and your sons do not follow your example, appoint a king over us, like all the nations, to rule us."

Samuel was displeased when they said, "Give us a king to rule us." But he prayed to the Lord. *The* Lord *said: Listen to whatever the people say. You are not the one they are rejecting. They are rejecting me as their king.*

Samuel delivered the message of the Lord *in full to those who were asking him for a king. He told them: "The governance of the king who will rule you will be as follows: He will take your sons and assign them to his chariots and horses, and they will run before his chariot. He will appoint from among them his commanders of thousands and of hundreds. He will make them do his plowing and harvesting and produce his weapons of war and chariotry. He will use your daughters as perfumers, cooks, and bakers.*

He will take your best fields, vineyards, and olive groves, and give them to his servants. He will tithe your crops and grape harvests to give to his officials and his servants. He will take your male and female slaves, as well as your best oxen and donkeys, and use them to do his work. He will also tithe your flocks. As for you, you will become his slaves. On that day you will cry out because of the king whom you have chosen, but the Lord will not answer you on that day."

The people, however, refused to listen to Samuel's warning and said, "No! There must be a king over us. We too must be like all the nations, with a king to rule us, lead us in warfare, and fight our battles." Samuel listened to all the concerns of the people and then repeated them to the Lord. The Lord said: Listen to them! Appoint a king to rule over them. Then Samuel said to the people of Israel, "Return, each one of you, to your own city."

Meditatio: God is well aware of the corruption that power brings. Instead of serving them, the kings will serve themselves. We often fall into the trap of thinking the right political leader will solve our problems for us. Yet each one seems to be worse than the last. They serve themselves instead of serving their people. Have we been faithful servants of Jesus, our king? Or have we wanted to be like the other nations? Read the passage a second time.

Oratio: The things we struggle with are often problems of our own making. Yet we are quick to point the finger at others or at God himself. Talk to God about what is on your heart. Then read the passage a third time, or just the part that struck you the most.

Contemplatio: God loves us and doesn't like to see us suffer or be oppressed. Spend a few minutes quietly receiving God's love for you and savoring his presence in your life.

SUGGESTIONS FOR JOURNALING
1. The part that most struck me from today's passage was …
2. I have experienced oppression when …

3. I have been guilty of serving myself when …
4. I reject God's lordship over me in the simple ways that I …
5. I sense God calling me to …

After you've journaled, close with a brief conversation with God giving thanks for your prayer experience. Then pray an Our Father.

January 17 — Saturday
Saturday of the First Week in Ordinary Time

SAINT ANTHONY, ABBOT, MEMORIAL

Anthony was born in Egypt around AD 251. At the age of eighteen or so, he was in a church and heard the Bible passage, "Go, sell what you have, and give to [the] poor and you will have treasure in heaven; then come, follow me" (Mk 10:21). He believed this was a personal invitation from God directed to him. He gave away his earthly possessions and went out into the desert to live a simple life of prayer and penance. During this period, the Church transitioned from a persecuted minority to a kind of state religion. Christianity became too easy and comfortable for many, who desired to give their all for Jesus. So, they went out into the desert and joined Anthony. He wrote a rule for them, which became the foundation of the monastic life.

REVIEW

Preparation: *Come, Holy Spirit, enlighten the eyes of my heart.* Call to mind his loving care for you and spend the first minute of your prayer just resting in the free, unearned gift of loving and being loved. Let gratitude rise in your heart.

We have just spent a week with the First Book of Samuel. We have seen some of the first steps that would ultimately lead to King David. You may not have realized that Samuel was the prophet that both called and anointed David. How have you experienced God's loving care for you this past week? When did challenges in your life lead to unexpected blessings? Here are some questions to help you:

1. Where did I notice God, and what was he doing or saying?
2. How did I respond to what God was doing?
3. I felt God's love most strongly when …
4. I found myself struggling with …
5. I'm grateful for …

6. Saturday of the First Week in Ordinary Time, my strongest sense, image, moment, or experience of God's loving presence was …

Conclude by conversing with God about your week. **Acknowledge** what you have been experiencing. **Relate** it to him. **Receive** what he wants to give you. **Respond** to him. Then savor that image of God's loving presence and rest there for a minute or two. Close with an Our Father.

Week Eight

Discernment of Spirits

"How do I know it's really God that is speaking to me?"

St. Ignatius of Loyola was a master of the discernment of spirits. He believes that we experience influence from both the Holy Spirit and also from the Devil, whom he refers to as "the enemy." The key to the discernment of spirits is to understand if the movement we are experiencing is coming from God or from the one who is opposed to God.

If we are generally living for ourselves and engaging in mortal sin, the enemy will try to keep us lulled into a false sense of security and comfort. For example, "Just a quick look at porn never hurt anyone." "You can quit drinking tomorrow. Tonight, enjoy yourself." For this kind of person, the work of the Good Spirit will feel like a slap in the face or an alarm clock (some people use the expression "spiritual 2 x 4"). The Holy Spirit needs to shake us out of our stupor so that we can see the danger to our soul.

On the other hand, if a person is generally trying to avoid sin, live for God, and grow in faith, this person will experience the opposite. Here, the enemy wants to interfere with our progress. He will propose imaginary obstacles, discouragements, distractions, and confusion. The voice of the enemy will be accusatory ("You're not good enough"; "You're broken"; "No one could love someone like you"; "You're doing it wrong; everyone else is having a better retreat than you"; "You missed a few days, you might as well quit, you could try again next year"). These thoughts come with feelings of unrest, fear, and sometimes panic. The Good Spirit, on the other hand, will be encouraging and supportive and come with a sense of peace. The Spirit will remind us that we are loved, valued, and forgiven. Even when we need a wake-up call, it will feel more like a gentle nudge.

Ignatius also points out the natural cycle of consolation and desolation. Consolation is when we can feel God's love and have a sense of peace and his presence; the right choices are obvious. Desolation is when we can't feel God's love, and instead we hear the voice of the enemy more strongly; right seems wrong, and bad choices come easily. Think of consolation like a sunny day and desolation like a dark and stormy night.

In desolation, we should not make a change, but keep walking on the road that we saw clearly when we were in consolation. In consolation, we should draw strength from God's love and prepare ourselves for when desolation comes again.

This pattern of easy and difficult, comfort and struggle, is to be expected on pilgrimages. Some days we feel strong and comforted, and we make progress easily. Other days are windy, cold, exhausting, and we find we have to put our heads down and just focus on putting one blistered foot in front of the other. The difficult times test your mettle and force you to face your fears and burdens. They are also the times with the most spiritual growth. So do not be discouraged if you have faced resistance, difficulties praying each day, and lots of struggles from inside of you and from outside. Resistance is a sign that you are on the right road and that, by overcoming obstacles, spiritual progress is happening. The only way to have a "bad pilgrimage" is to quit. Just keep walking, however slowly it may be, and you will eventually reach your goal.

Grace of the Week: We continue our adventure with the daily readings from the Mass. We will mediate on the fall of King Saul and the rise of King David. Ask God for the grace to live your own calling with humility and courage.

January 18 — Sunday
Second Sunday in Ordinary Time

Preparation: *Come, Holy Spirit, enlighten the eyes of my heart.* Be present to the God who is always present to you. Call to mind his loving care for you and spend the first minute of your prayer just resting in the free, unearned gift of loving and being loved. Let gratitude rise in your heart.

Lectio: Ask God for the grace to live your own calling with humility and courage. Today we will meditate on the extended version of the first reading from the lectionary. This is one of four passages from Isaiah that refer to a mysterious Servant of the Lord (see Is 42:1–9; 49:1–7; 50:4–9; 52:13—53:12). The servant is identified as "Israel" (which could refer to the whole people), who by doing God's work shows forth his glory. But then, later on in the passage, the servant is identified as one who brings back Jacob and restores Israel (Jacob and Israel are two names for the same person, the grandson of Abraham and the father of the "twelve tribes of Israel"). Who is this mysterious figure? Read the passage slowly and prayerfully.

ISAIAH 49:1–6

Hear me, coastlands,
  listen, distant peoples.
*Before birth the L*ORD *called me,*
  from my mother's womb he gave me my name.
He made my mouth like a sharp-edged sword,
  concealed me, shielded by his hand.
He made me a sharpened arrow,
  in his quiver he hid me.
He said to me, You are my servant,
  in you, Israel, I show my glory.

Though I thought I had toiled in vain,

> for nothing and for naught spent my strength,
> Yet my right is with the Lord,
>   my recompense is with my God.
> For now the Lord has spoken
>   who formed me as his servant from the womb,
> That Jacob may be brought back to him
>   and Israel gathered to him;
> I am honored in the sight of the Lord,
>   and my God is now my strength!
> It is too little, he says, for you to be my servant,
>   to raise up the tribes of Jacob,
>   and restore the survivors of Israel;
> I will make you a light to the nations,
>   that my salvation may reach to the ends of the earth.

Meditatio: Early Christians recognized in Isaiah's mysterious Servant of the Lord prophecies referring to Jesus Christ. Jesus saves the people, and in doing so becomes the leader of God's holy people, the Church. We are each called to not only receive salvation from Christ, but also to show God's glory by our faithful service to the King. What does this passage say about Jesus the Servant of the Lord? How does this passage call me to be a more faithful servant of the Lord? Notice whatever word or phrase stands out to you as you read the passage a second time.

Oratio: God formed you in the womb and knew your name before you were born. He has been sharpening you for your special mission, concealing you in his quiver. How did Jesus prepare for his mission? How are you called to participate in Jesus' mission of salvation? What special gift, blessing, or task has God assigned to you? Ask God these questions. If you find yourself afraid, feeling like you have spent your strength for nothing, or convinced that you couldn't possibly have a special mission, talk to God about that as well. Be open and honest with him.

Contemplatio: Read the passage a third time. This time just receive whatever God wants to give you. Perhaps he will invite you to a new way of seeing, thinking, or believing. Perhaps he will remind you of a past prayer time, experience, or encounter that speaks of your mission and purpose. Be open to receive whatever God wants to give you. Sometimes our own goodness is the hardest thing to believe in. Be with the Lord who loves you, and enjoy this time together. Savor his presence for a minute or two before moving on.

SUGGESTIONS FOR JOURNALING

1. The part of the prophecy that most spoke to me was …
2. My strongest thought, feeling, or desire was …
3. I have a hard time believing that …
4. I noticed God's presence most strongly …
5. What part do I play in bringing God's salvation to the ends of the earth?

January 18 — Sunday

After you've journaled, close with a brief conversation giving thanks to God for your prayer experience. Then pray an Our Father.

January 19 — Monday
Monday of the Second Week in Ordinary Time

Preparation: *Come, Holy Spirit, enlighten the eyes of my heart.* Be present to the God who is always present to you. Call to mind his loving care for you and spend the first minute of your prayer just resting in the free, unearned gift of loving and being loved. Let gratitude rise in your heart.

Lectio: Ask God for the grace to live your own calling with humility and courage. Samuel was a great prophet and led the people well. But his sons took bribes, just like Eli's sons had done. So, the people approached Samuel and insisted they be given a king (see 1 Sm 8). Samuel anointed Saul, who was tall and handsome. He fit the appearances of a king. However, he was also vain and self-serving. He was more worried about what people thought of him and of being successful than he was concerned for following God's will. Read the passage slowly and prayerfully.

1 SAMUEL 15:16–23 (LECTIONARY)
Samuel said to Saul:
*"Stop! Let me tell you what the L*ORD *said to me last night."*
Saul replied, "Speak!"
Samuel then said: "Though little in your own esteem,
are you not leader of the tribes of Israel?
*The L*ORD *anointed you king of Israel and sent you on a*
*   mission, saying,*
'Go and put the sinful Amalekites under a ban of destruc-
*   tion.*
Fight against them until you have exterminated them.'
*Why then have you disobeyed the L*ORD*?*
*You have pounced on the spoil, thus displeasing the L*ORD*."*
*Saul answered Samuel: "I did indeed obey the L*ORD
*and fulfill the mission on which the L*ORD *sent me.*
I have brought back Agag, and I have destroyed Amalek

> under the ban.
> But from the spoil the men took sheep and oxen,
> the best of what had been banned,
> to sacrifice to the LORD their God in Gilgal."
> But Samuel said:
> "Does the LORD so delight in burnt offerings and sacrifices
> as in obedience to the command of the LORD?
> Obedience is better than sacrifice,
> and submission than the fat of rams.
> For a sin like divination is rebellion,
> and presumption is the crime of idolatry.
> Because you have rejected the command of the LORD,
> he, too, has rejected you as ruler."

Meditatio: Looting your enemies' stuff was a major part of ancient battles (and many modern video games). The Israelite soldiers were forbidden from making a profit in their battle against their sinful enemies; everything must be destroyed. Saul has decided to bend the rules, and Samuel is not impressed. The people must obey their king, but the king must obey God. Have you ever invented a clever justification for creatively disregarding God's rules?

Oratio: There has been a long struggle between God's Chosen People and the neighboring nations who practice witchcraft, idolatry, and ritual prostitution. The Bible presents this struggle in terms of Israel learning to serve God and resist the temptation to serve idols and behave like their pagan neighbors. I don't want you to get caught up in the "holy war" aspect of this passage. Many Church Fathers believed that these passages were meant to tell Christians to put to death any false worship or sinful behavior within our own hearts. Notice the key concept of faithful obedience versus doing whatever seems good to the king and his men. I think this concept continues to be very relevant today. Read the passage a second time and notice your own feelings. Do you find obedience to God's law difficult sometimes? Talk to God about it. You can be honest without fear that he will smite you.

***Contemplatio*:** Read the passage a third time. This time just receive whatever God wants to give you. Be assured that his will comes from a place of loving you and wanting whatever is best for you. Rest for a few minutes in whatever way he reveals his presence to you in your prayer time today.

SUGGESTIONS FOR JOURNALING
1. I was particularly moved or inspired by …
2. I had a hard time accepting that …
3. God was with me, and he wanted me to know …
4. I received a new insight or perspective that …
5. I need to make a change in my life …

244 *January 19 — Monday*

After you've journaled, close with a brief conversation giving thanks to God for his presence with you in prayer today. Then pray an Our Father.

January 20 — Tuesday
Tuesday of the Second Week in Ordinary Time

Preparation: *Come, Holy Spirit, enlighten the eyes of my heart.* Be present to the God who is always present to you. Call to mind his loving care for you and spend the first minute of your prayer just resting in the free, unearned gift of loving and being loved. Let gratitude rise in your heart.

Set the Scene: Ask God for the grace to live your own calling with humility and courage. Saul could only expect obedience from his people if he himself was willing to submit to God's authority. He rejected God first before God rejected him. Notice that Saul is now using his kingly power to protect himself (as Herod will), and Samuel is afraid of him. God provides him with a reason for his visit so he can "fly under the radar" of King Saul. Picture a courtyard in the center of the town of Bethlehem. A sacrifice was also a sacred meal, and the town is invited. Even Samuel doesn't know exactly how this will go. Read the passage slowly and prayerfully.

1 SAMUEL 16:1–13 (LECTIONARY)

*The L*ORD *said to Samuel:*
"How long will you grieve for Saul,
whom I have rejected as king of Israel?
Fill your horn with oil, and be on your way.
I am sending you to Jesse of Bethlehem,
for I have chosen my king from among his sons."
But Samuel replied:
"How can I go?
Saul will hear of it and kill me."
*To this the L*ORD *answered:*
"Take a heifer along and say,
*'I have come to sacrifice to the L*ORD*.'*
Invite Jesse to the sacrifice, and I myself will tell you what
*   to do;*

you are to anoint for me the one I point out to you."

Samuel did as the Lord had commanded him.
When he entered Bethlehem,
the elders of the city came trembling to meet him and inquired,
"Is your visit peaceful, O seer?"
He replied:
"Yes! I have come to sacrifice to the Lord.
So cleanse yourselves and join me today for the banquet."
He also had Jesse and his sons cleanse themselves
and invited them to the sacrifice.
As they came, he looked at Eliab and thought,
"Surely the Lord's anointed is here before him."
But the Lord said to Samuel:
"Do not judge from his appearance or from his lofty stature,
because I have rejected him.
Not as man sees does God see,
because he sees the appearance
but the Lord looks into the heart."
Then Jesse called Abinadab and presented him before Samuel,
who said, "The Lord has not chosen him."
Next Jesse presented Shammah, but Samuel said,
"The Lord has not chosen this one either."
In the same way Jesse presented seven sons before Samuel,
but Samuel said to Jesse,
"The Lord has not chosen any one of these."
Then Samuel asked Jesse,
"Are these all the sons you have?"
Jesse replied,
"There is still the youngest, who is tending the sheep."
Samuel said to Jesse,
"Send for him;

> we will not begin the sacrificial banquet until he arrives here."
> Jesse sent and had the young man brought to them.
> He was ruddy, a youth handsome to behold
> and making a splendid appearance.
> The LORD said,
> "There—anoint him, for this is he!"
> Then Samuel, with the horn of oil in hand,
> anointed him in the midst of his brothers;
> and from that day on, the Spirit of the LORD rushed upon David.
> When Samuel took his leave, he went to Ramah.

Action! The youngest boy is too unimportant to invite to the feast. He is out tending sheep, a lowly task. God is casting down the mighty from their thrones and raising up the lowly. How does Samuel feel when Jesse runs out of sons? How do the brothers feel when their youngest brother is chosen over the rest of them? Play the scene forward in your mind.

Acknowledge: Read the passage a second time. Notice what is going on in your own heart. Have you ever felt passed over by others? Have you ever felt especially chosen by God?

Relate: Turn to God and share with him what is on your heart. Would you welcome the Spirit of God if it rushed upon you? Perhaps ask God to stir into flames the Spirit you received at baptism and confirmation. Tell him whatever you are thinking.

Receive: Read the passage a third time. Now just receive whatever God wants to give you — a sense that he is listening, his loving presence with you, peace, courage, a calling, or something else.

Respond: Say yes to whatever God desires to give you in this moment. The same God who chose David has also chosen you. Rest in his loving care for a few minutes before moving on.

SUGGESTIONS FOR JOURNALING
1. What jumped out at me from this passage was …
2. The Spirit of God felt particularly strong when …
3. I struggled to understand or receive …
4. I felt God reminding me, calling me, or inviting me …
5. I ended prayer with a conviction that …

Tuesday of the Second Week in Ordinary Time **249**

After you've journaled, close with a brief conversation of thanksgiving to God for his presence with you in prayer today. Then pray an Our Father.

January 21 — Wednesday
Wednesday of the Second Week in Ordinary Time

SAINT AGNES, VIRGIN AND MARTYR, MEMORIAL
Tradition holds that Agnes was a young Roman noblewoman martyred under the Emperor Diocletian around the year 304. She is one of seven women mentioned by name in the Roman Canon of the Mass (Eucharistic Prayer I). Her name comes from the Latin word *agnus* meaning "lamb." She is often depicted holding a lamb in witness to the innocence of her youth and virginity. On this day in Rome, the Holy Father blesses two sheep whose wool will be woven into the pallia worn by archbishops.

Preparation: *Come, Holy Spirit, enlighten the eyes of my heart.* Be present to the God who is always present to you. Call to mind his loving care for you and spend the first minute of your prayer just resting in the free, unearned gift of loving and being loved. Let gratitude rise in your heart.

Set the Scene: Ask God for the grace to live your own calling with humility and courage. Today's passage is one of the most famous scenes in the Bible. David's three oldest brothers are serving in Saul's army. David is running food from the family homestead on Bethlehem to his brothers on the front line. A gigantic Philistine warrior has been taunting the Israelites to man-to-man combat, but no one will take the field against him. Read the passage and picture the swords, spears, and scimitars (a curved sword) of ancient warfare as you read this passage.

1 SAMUEL 17:32–33, 37, 40–51 (LECTIONARY)
> David spoke to Saul:
> "Let your majesty not lose courage.
>   I am at your service to go and fight this Philistine."
> But Saul answered David,
> "You cannot go up against this Philistine and fight with him,

for you are only a youth, while he has been a warrior from
    his youth."

David continued:
"The LORD, who delivered me from the claws of the lion
    and the bear,
will also keep me safe from the clutches of this Philistine."
Saul answered David, "Go! the LORD will be with you."

Then, staff in hand, David selected five smooth stones
    from the wadi
    and put them in the pocket of his shepherd's bag.
With his sling also ready to hand, he approached the
    Philistine.

With his shield bearer marching before him,
the Philistine also advanced closer and closer to David.
When he had sized David up,
and seen that he was youthful, and ruddy, and handsome
    in appearance,
the Philistine held David in contempt.
The Philistine said to David,
"Am I a dog that you come against me with a staff?"
Then the Philistine cursed David by his gods
and said to him, "Come here to me,
    and I will leave your flesh for the birds of the air
and the beasts of the field."
David answered him:
"You come against me with sword and spear and scimitar,
but I come against you in the name of the LORD of hosts,
the God of the armies of Israel that you have insulted.
Today the LORD shall deliver you into my hand;
I will strike you down and cut off your head.
This very day I will leave your corpse
and the corpses of the Philistine army for the birds of the
    air

and the beasts of the field;
thus the whole land shall learn that Israel has a God.
All this multitude, too,
shall learn that it is not by sword or spear that the Lord *saves.*
For the battle is the Lord's *and he shall deliver you into our hands."*

The Philistine then moved to meet David at close quarters,
while David ran quickly toward the battle line
in the direction of the Philistine.
David put his hand into the bag and took out a stone,
hurled it with the sling,
and struck the Philistine on the forehead.
The stone embedded itself in his brow,
and he fell prostrate on the ground.
Thus David overcame the Philistine with sling and stone;
he struck the Philistine mortally, and did it without a sword.
Then David ran and stood over him;
with the Philistine's own sword which he drew from its sheath
he dispatched him and cut off his head.

Action! Imagine both sides watching as this obviously lopsided battle unfolds. The head on Goliath's spear weighs fifteen pounds, and his chain mail coat weighs 125 pounds (see 1 Sm 17:4–7). David is dressed as a shepherd with a staff and sling; he probably doesn't weigh much more than Goliath's armor. David is armed with confidence that God is with him and God will win the victory through him. In what way is David an image of Christ?

Acknowledge: Read the passage a second time. Notice what is going on inside of you. Have you ever found yourself in a lopsided fight? Did you trust in God? What happened?

Relate: The God who protected David is also with you now. Share with him whatever is on your heart. It can be particularly hard if the outcome wasn't what you expected. Perhaps your experience was less like David's and more like Jesus on the cross. Be honest with God your Father about whatever you need to say. Don't hold anything back.

Receive: Read the passage a third time. This time, be open to whatever God wants to communicate to you. Let yourself be open to seeing things from God's perspective.

Respond: The same God who was with David is also with you. Respond to whatever he has given you, then rest in his loving care for a few minutes before moving on.

SUGGESTIONS FOR JOURNALING
1. The detail that most spoke to me was …
2. The story of David and Goliath reminded me of …
3. God wanted me to know that …
4. I ended prayer with a new sense that …
5. What would it look like for me to face my daily struggles with the same faith in God that David had?

254 *January 21 — Wednesday*

After you've journaled, close with a brief conversation thanking God for whatever happened in today's prayer time today. Then pray an Our Father.

January 22 — Thursday
Thursday of the Second Week in Ordinary Time

DAY OF PRAYER FOR THE LEGAL PROTECTION OF UNBORN CHILDREN (USA)

In the United States of America, January 22 shall be observed as a particular day of penance for violations to the dignity of the human person committed through acts of abortion, and of prayer for the full restoration of the legal guarantee to the right to life. Do some extra prayer or penance today.

Preparation: *Come, Holy Spirit, enlighten the eyes of my heart.* Be present to the God who is always present to you. Call to mind his loving care for you and spend the first minute of your prayer just resting in the free, unearned gift of loving and being loved. Let gratitude rise in your heart.

Lectio: Ask God for the grace to live your own calling with humility and courage. The Bible makes it clear that those who choose to follow God will face opposition. Saul's house is divided. The king is trapped in self-protection and sees David as a potential threat to the throne. His son Jonathan is great friends with David and tries to change his father's mind. Read the passage slowly and prayerfully.

1 SAMUEL 18:6–9; 19:1–7 (LECTIONARY)

When David and Saul approached
(on David's return after slaying the Philistine),
women came out from each of the cities of Israel to meet King Saul,
singing and dancing, with tambourines, joyful songs, and sistrums.
The women played and sang:

"Saul has slain his thousands,
and David his ten thousands."

Saul was very angry and resentful of the song, for he thought:
"They give David ten thousands, but only thousands to me.
All that remains for him is the kingship."
And from that day on, Saul was jealous of David.

Saul discussed his intention of killing David
with his son Jonathan and with all his servants.
But Saul's son Jonathan, who was very fond of David, told him:
"My father Saul is trying to kill you.
Therefore, please be on your guard tomorrow morning;
get out of sight and remain in hiding.
I, however, will go out and stand beside my father
in the countryside where you are, and will speak to him about you.
If I learn anything, I will let you know."

Jonathan then spoke well of David to his father Saul, saying to him:
"Let not your majesty sin against his servant David,
for he has committed no offense against you,
but has helped you very much by his deeds.
When he took his life in his hands and slew the Philistine,
and the LORD brought about a great victory
for all Israel through him,
you were glad to see it.
Why, then, should you become guilty of shedding innocent blood
by killing David without cause?"
Saul heeded Jonathan's plea and swore,
"As the LORD lives, he shall not be killed."
So Jonathan summoned David and repeated the whole conversation to him.
Jonathan then brought David to Saul, and David served him as before.

Meditatio: Have you had a friend like Jonathan, one who was even willing to stand up to his powerful king dad on your behalf? Have you been a friend like this to someone else? Have you found yourself like Saul trying to stave off a potential rival? Despite Saul's power, he still feels insecure. Reflect on what was going on in the heart of each of the key figures in this passage.

Oratio: Read the passage again. Notice what moves in your own heart, then share it with God. Speak to him about the places where you pursue self-protection, or your gratitude for a friendship like that of David and Jonathan's, or your longing for such a friend.

Contemplatio: Read the passage a third time, or just the part that most spoke to you. This time just receive whatever God wants to give you. Know that you are special to him and that God values your friendship. Rest for a few minutes in whatever way he reveals his presence to you in your prayer time today.

SUGGESTIONS FOR JOURNALING
1. What I noticed about Saul was …
2. I was particularly inspired by …
3. I found myself wanting …
4. God was with me, and he wanted me to know …
5. I ended prayer with …

258 *January 22 — Thursday*

After you've journaled, close with a brief conversation giving thanks to God for his friendship with you and for the other good friends in your life. Then pray an Our Father.

January 23 — Friday
Friday of the Second Week in Ordinary Time

Preparation: *Come, Holy Spirit, enlighten the eyes of my heart.* Be present to the God who is always present to you. Call to mind his loving care for you and spend the first minute of your prayer just resting in the free, unearned gift of loving and being loved. Let gratitude rise in your heart.

Set the Scene: Ask God for the grace to live your own calling with humility and courage. For the next couple of years, Saul moves back and forth between tolerating David and trying to kill him. David ends up something like Robin Hood, a hunted outlaw with a band of men following him. Picture the wild goat crags, some of which are used by shepherds for their sheep, as you read this passage.

1 SAMUEL 24:3–21 (LECTIONARY)

*Saul took three thousand picked men from all Israel
and went in search of David and his men
in the direction of the wild goat crags.
When he came to the sheepfolds along the way, he found
    a cave,
which he entered to relieve himself.
David and his men were occupying the inmost recesses of
    the cave.*

*David's servants said to him,
"This is the day of which the* Lord *said to you,
'I will deliver your enemy into your grasp;
do with him as you see fit.'"
So David moved up and stealthily cut off an end of Saul's
    mantle.
Afterward, however, David regretted that he had cut off
    an end of Saul's mantle.*

He said to his men,
"The Lord forbid that I should do such a thing to my master,
the Lord's anointed, as to lay a hand on him,
for he is the Lord's anointed."
With these words David restrained his men
and would not permit them to attack Saul.
Saul then left the cave and went on his way.
David also stepped out of the cave, calling to Saul,
"My lord the king!"
When Saul looked back, David bowed to the ground in homage and asked Saul:
"Why do you listen to those who say,
'David is trying to harm you'?
You see for yourself today that the Lord just now delivered you
into my grasp in the cave.
I had some thought of killing you, but I took pity on you instead.
I decided, 'I will not raise a hand against my lord,
for he is the Lord's anointed and a father to me.'
Look here at this end of your mantle which I hold.
Since I cut off an end of your mantle and did not kill you,
see and be convinced that I plan no harm and no rebellion.
I have done you no wrong,
though you are hunting me down to take my life.
The Lord will judge between me and you,
and the Lord will exact justice from you in my case.
I shall not touch you.
The old proverb says, 'From the wicked comes forth wickedness.'
So I will take no action against you.
Against whom are you on campaign, O king of Israel?
Whom are you pursuing? A dead dog, or a single flea!
The Lord will be the judge; he will decide between me and you.

> *May he see this, and take my part,*
> *and grant me justice beyond your reach!"*
>
> *When David finished saying these things to Saul, Saul answered,*
> *"Is that your voice, my son David?"*
> *And Saul wept aloud.*
> *Saul then said to David: "You are in the right rather than I;*
> *you have treated me generously, while I have done you harm.*
> *Great is the generosity you showed me today,*
> *when the* Lord *delivered me into your grasp*
> *and you did not kill me.*
> *For if a man meets his enemy, does he send him away unharmed?*
> *May the* Lord *reward you generously for what you have done this day.*
> *And now, I know that you shall surely be king*
> *and that sovereignty over Israel shall come into your possession."*

Action! Saul is trapped in self-protection. David's trust in God leads him to a very different attitude toward this conflict. Saul's army of three thousand picked men against David's small band is a replay of the David-and-Goliath story. Have you gotten the point yet?

Acknowledge: Place yourself in the scene. Where are you? What are you feeling and thinking? Read the passage a second time.

Relate: Turn to God. Speak to him from your heart. Can you trust him as David does, or do you still struggle to believe that God will protect you and provide for you? Say whatever you are feeling with complete honesty.

Receive: Read the passage a third time. How does God respond to what you have shared with him?

Respond: Receive God's loving care for you here and now. Let go of your worries, fears, and concerns and just be with him for a few minutes before you look at the suggestions for journaling.

SUGGESTIONS FOR JOURNALING
1. The main thing I got from today's reading was …
2. If I trust God, then I will …
3. I see more clearly that David is a picture of Jesus Christ in the way he …
4. God is calling me to …
5. I need to respond by …

After you've journaled, close with thanksgiving to God for the gift of today's prayer experience. End with an Our Father.

January 24 — Saturday
Saturday of the Second Week in Ordinary Time

ST. FRANCIS DE SALES, MEMORIAL

Born August 21, 1567, Francis was the son of a senator from the province of Savoy in France. His father sent him to study law in preparation to follow in his own footsteps. Francis, however, felt a call to become a priest. He patiently and gently won his father's consent. Part of his conversion happened when he heard a Calvinist preach on predestination and became convinced that he was predestined for eternal damnation. Eventually, he came to experience God's love for him and realized a loving God would not predestine anyone to hell. He was an effective preacher himself and converted many Calvinists back to the Catholic Faith. At the age of thirty-five, he was named bishop of Geneva, then being run as an autocratic theocracy by none other than John Calvin himself. He spent twenty years conquering his quick temper, so much so that he became famous for his gentle character. His many pamphlets on the Faith, famous books, and exhaustive correspondence made him a patron of the Catholic press.

REVIEW

Preparation: *Come, Holy Spirit, enlighten the eyes of my heart.* Call to mind God's loving care for you and spend the first minute of your prayer just resting in the free, unearned gift of loving and being loved.

Our Scripture passages this past week gave us some powerful and memorable images of what trusting God could look like. Let's review those prayer periods and try to draw out some of the blessings we received. Here are some questions to help you:

1. Where did I notice God, and what was he doing or saying?
2. How did I respond to what God was doing?
3. I felt God's love most strongly when …
4. I found myself struggling with …

5. I'm grateful for …
6. This past week, my strongest sense, image, moment, or experience of God's loving presence was …
7. What would my life look like if I lived with the faith and trust of David?

Conclude by conversing with God about your week. **Acknowledge** what you have been experiencing. **Relate** it to him. **Receive** what he wants to give you. **Respond** to him. Then savor that image of God's loving presence and rest there for a minute or two. Close with an Our Father.

Week Nine

Relational Prayer (ARRR)

We have learned two forms of prayer, *Lectio Divina* and Imaginative Prayer. I want to teach you a third prayer form, called relational prayer or "A-R-R-R." You've already seen this prayer form as part of imaginative prayer. Let's review the four steps:

Acknowledge what is going on inside of you — your thoughts, feelings, and desires.
Relate, or share with the Lord what is going on inside of you.
Receive what God wants to give you.
Respond to what the Lord just gave you.

This prayer form can stand on its own as a way of praying with the experiences of everyday life. Let's say I'm in on the phone with a relative who is upset that my family's plans for Christmas don't fit her expectations. She implies that, "Some people need to learn to be more flexible; they can't just expect the rest of the world to revolve around them." I get angry and say something like "Do you have any idea how difficult it is to juggle all the different holiday get-togethers?" "I'm just saying," she says, "I hope you all have yourselves a nice Christmas." And that's the end of the conversation. I hang up and yell, "By 'being flexible' you really mean the rest of the world is supposed to revolve around you!"

Great. Now I've lost the Christmas spirit, and I'm going to be angry the rest of the day. "Does she have any idea how hard I work to make everyone happy, and no one's ever happy." I could stew on it or I could let God help me. So, I go sit in my prayer corner or just focus on God wherever I happen to be. I start, as we always do: "Come Holy Spirit, enlighten the eyes of my heart." I call to mind God's loving care for me that I experienced in a recent prayer time and let gratitude rise in my heart. I'm still feeling angry, but I know I'm not alone. Next, I **Acknowledge** what is going on inside of me. Why am I angry? I notice the feelings that happened before I got angry, such as feeling unappreciated or disrespected or not valued, or that I was tired and overwhelmed with scheduling. I might realize I have a wound in this area that makes these kinds of conversations hurt more than they should.

Now I turn to Jesus and focus on him. I could also speak to God the Father, the Holy Spirit, or Mother Mary. It might help to call to mind a favorite image, such as the Good Shepherd or Divine Mercy or one of the memorable moments when Jesus and I connected through imaginative prayer. I **Relate** what I'm feeling and share my heart with him. The important thing here is that my focus needs to shift from me and my problem to the Lord. First, it was me looking at my problem, then both of us looking at my problem, and now I'm looking at him. I **Receive** what he wants to give me: a feeling, a thought, a reminder, a Scripture passage, and the like. I also might realize things about myself. Perhaps I tend to be a pleaser, or I was already frustrated by something else before the conversation even started. I **Respond** by acting out of this new vision by letting go of something or resolving to handle things differently next time with Jesus' help. I might need to pray for her or forgive her. I might need to forgive myself. I end with gratitude to God.

Try it for yourself at some point this week. You will be surprised how much this simple prayer form will change your life. Sharing your burdens with God makes them shrink like snow in the sunshine.

Grace of the Week: This week is our last full week of *Oriens*. Inspired by Sunday's Gospel, we will focus on the call of discipleship. Ask God for the grace to hear him calling you and to follow him faithfully in your daily life.

January 25 — Sunday
Third Sunday in Ordinary Time

Preparation: *Come, Holy Spirit, enlighten the eyes of my heart.* Be present to the God who is always present to you. Call to mind his loving care for you and spend the first minute of your prayer just resting in the free, unearned gift of loving and being loved. Let gratitude rise in your heart.

Set the Scene: Ask God for the grace to hear him calling you and to follow him faithfully in your daily life. The Sea of Galilee is a large freshwater lake. It sits about twenty miles east of Nazareth, Jesus' hometown. Matthew depicts Jesus' decision to start preaching in this area as a fulfillment of Old Testament prophecy. Use your imagination to see the fishing boats, smell the sea, and hear the gulls calling overhead.

MATTHEW 4:12–23 (LECTIONARY)
*When Jesus heard that John had been arrested,
he withdrew to Galilee.
He left Nazareth and went to live in Capernaum by the sea,
in the region of Zebulun and Naphtali,
that what had been said through Isaiah the prophet
might be fulfilled:
Land of Zebulun and land of Naphtali,
the way to the sea, beyond the Jordan,
Galilee of the Gentiles,
the people who sit in darkness have seen a great light,
on those dwelling in a land overshadowed by death
light has arisen.
From that time on, Jesus began to preach and say,
"Repent, for the kingdom of heaven is at hand."*

As he was walking by the Sea of Galilee, he saw two brothers,

Simon who is called Peter, and his brother Andrew,
casting a net into the sea; they were fishermen.
He said to them,
"Come after me, and I will make you fishers of men."
At once they left their nets and followed him.
He walked along from there and saw two other brothers,
James, the son of Zebedee, and his brother John.
They were in a boat, with their father Zebedee, mending their nets.
He called them, and immediately they left their boat and their father
and followed him.
He went around all of Galilee,
teaching in their synagogues, proclaiming the gospel of the kingdom,
curing every disease and illness among the people.

Action! Jesus was just baptized by John in the Jordan River, which flows south out of the Sea of Galilee (see Mt 3:13–16). Then he spent forty days in the desert (4:1–12). Now he picks up the torch left by John as he proclaims, "Repent, for the kingdom of heaven is at hand." What made the first disciples decide to follow him? What was it like for them to hear Jesus preach and then see him cure diseases and illnesses among the people?

Acknowledge: Last week we watched as Saul tried to use his power and position to protect himself from a perceived rival. This week we watch four fisherman trust Jesus enough to walk away from their livelihoods. What made them trust Jesus enough to walk away from the life they had known? How did you feel as you watched them? Read the passage a second time.

Relate: Find a quiet spot and sit with Jesus. Share your thoughts, feelings, and desires with him. Are you afraid of what he might call you to, or are you perhaps thinking "Jesus would never call me"? Be completely honest; he already knows, he's just waiting for you to open your heart to him.

Receive: Is there something Jesus wants you to know? Open your heart to him and receive whatever he wants to share with you. Read the passage a third time.

Respond: Receive God's loving care for you here and now. Let go of your worries, fears, and concerns and just be with him for a few minutes. The primary call of a vocation is not to go do something or be something, but first and foremost to be with the Lord. Answer that call by being with the Lord for a few minutes.

SUGGESTIONS FOR JOURNALING
1. I was struck by …
2. Following Jesus and leaving everything behind feels like …
3. I sensed Jesus was with me and he wanted me to know …
4. God is calling me to …
5. Being with him more closely in my daily life would look like …

274 *January 25 — Sunday*

After you've journaled, close with a short little prayer of thanks and gratitude, then pray one Our Father.

January 26 — Monday
Monday of the Third Week in Ordinary Time

SAINTS TIMOTHY AND TITUS, BISHOPS, MEMORIAL
Saint Timothy was the son of a pagan father and a Hebrew-Christian mother named Eunice (see 2 Tm 1:5). He was a disciple of Saint Paul and accompanied him on his journeys. Paul consecrated him bishop of Ephesus. An early legend says he was killed by a pagan mob when he opposed a pagan festival. Saint Titus was also a friend and disciple of Paul, who ordained him bishop of Crete. Paul wrote three pastoral letters to these two disciples. January 25 is the feast of the Conversion of Saint Paul, and the next day (today) we celebrate the feasts of two men whom Paul mentored in the Christian life.

Preparation: *Come, Holy Spirit, enlighten the eyes of my heart.* Be present to the God who is always present to you. Call to mind his loving care for you and spend the first minute of your prayer just resting in the free, unearned gift of loving and being loved. Let gratitude rise in your heart.

Lectio: Ask God for the grace to hear him calling you and to follow him faithfully in your daily life. Timothy and Titus were both disciples of Saint Paul. He wrote letters to encourage them in their ministry. As you read this passage, picture Timothy weighed down by the cares of his Christian community in Ephesus, the controversies over false teachings, and the sometimes-difficult relationships with the neighboring Jews and pagans. A messenger arrives bearing a letter from Rome. Paul, his old mentor and spiritual father, has sent him comfort and counsel. Imagine the scene as Timothy unrolls the letter and begins to read. What time of day is it? Where is he sitting? What goes on in his heart as he reads these words?

2 TIMOTHY 1:1–8 (LECTIONARY)
Paul, an Apostle of Christ Jesus by the will of God for the promise of life in Christ Jesus,

to Timothy, my dear child:
grace, mercy, and peace from God the Father
and Christ Jesus our Lord.

I am grateful to God,
whom I worship with a clear conscience as my ancestors did,
as I remember you constantly in my prayers, night and day.
I yearn to see you again, recalling your tears,
so that I may be filled with joy,
as I recall your sincere faith
that first lived in your grandmother Lois
and in your mother Eunice
and that I am confident lives also in you.

For this reason, I remind you to stir into flame
the gift of God that you have through the imposition of my hands.
For God did not give us a spirit of cowardice
but rather of power and love and self-control.
So do not be ashamed of your testimony to our Lord,
nor of me, a prisoner for his sake;
but bear your share of hardship for the Gospel
with the strength that comes from God.

Meditatio: We all need both a Paul and a Timothy. We need someone to mentor us in our faith and equip us for ministry; we need to mentor someone else in the Faith. Who has been like a Paul to you? Who is your Timothy? All Scripture is inspired by God. The God who loves you guided Paul, through the Holy Spirit, to write these words to you. What is God saying to you? Read the passage again.

Oratio: Now speak to God about what speaks to you. Raise your mind and heart to God. Talk to him about the struggles you are experiencing on the road of discipleship.

Contemplatio: Read the passage a third time. Receive what is in God's heart for you, his thoughts and feelings and desires for you, his child. Spend some time resting in God's loving care for you.

SUGGESTIONS FOR JOURNALING
1. The word, phrase, or idea that most spoke to me was …
2. What I really needed today was …
3. God wanted me to know …
4. I ended prayer wanting …
5. Who has been a Paul for me? Who has been a Timothy?
6. Discipleship means to me …

278 *January 26 — Monday*

After you've journaled, close with gratitude to God for his loving care for you in today's prayer and all through this *Oriens* pilgrimage. Then pray an Our Father.

January 27 — Tuesday
Tuesday of the Third Week in Ordinary Time

Preparation: *Come, Holy Spirit, enlighten the eyes of my heart.* Be present to the God who is always present to you. Call to mind his loving care for you and spend the first minute of your prayer just resting in the free, unearned gift of loving and being loved. Let gratitude rise in your heart.

Lectio: Ask God for the grace to hear him calling you and to follow him faithfully in your daily life. The call to follow Jesus is not fundamentally a call to go somewhere or do something. It is a call to *be with Jesus* and to *learn from him.* The first thing we learn from being with Jesus is his absolute trust in and dependence on his Father in heaven. Jesus wants us to share his faith. Read the passage slowly and prayerfully.

MATTHEW 6:24–34

"No one can serve two masters. He will either hate one and love the other, or be devoted to one and despise the other. You cannot serve God and mammon.

"Therefore I tell you, do not worry about your life, what you will eat [or drink], or about your body, what you will wear. Is not life more than food and the body more than clothing? Look at the birds in the sky; they do not sow or reap, they gather nothing into barns, yet your heavenly Father feeds them. Are not you more important than they? Can any of you by worrying add a single moment to your life-span? Why are you anxious about clothes? Learn from the way the wild flowers grow. They do not work or spin. But I tell you that not even Solomon in all his splendor was clothed like one of them. If God so clothes the grass of the field, which grows today and is thrown into the oven tomorrow, will he not much more provide for you, O you of little faith? So do not worry and

> say, 'What are we to eat?' or 'What are we to drink?' or 'What are we to wear?' All these things the pagans seek. Your heavenly Father knows that you need them all. But seek first the kingdom [of God] and his righteousness, and all these things will be given you besides. Do not worry about tomorrow; tomorrow will take care of itself. Sufficient for a day is its own evil."

Meditatio: Does this passage seem too good to be true? On my thirty-day silent retreat, I forgot to bring a backpack. I was visiting the chapel each day and carried my Bible, journal, and spiritual reading in a plastic grocery bag. I prayed with this passage, and I heard it as a personal invitation to trust the Father. Still, I pointed out to my spiritual director that it wasn't like a book bag would fall from the sky. That afternoon I walked to Goodwill and purchased a nice little book bag at a discount price. I washed it in my bathtub and hung it up to dry so it would be ready to use the next day. The next morning I discovered, sitting right in front of my door, a brand-new backpack, so new that it still had the tags on it. A note from a fellow retreatant said he noticed me carrying my books in a grocery bag, and he had this backpack he didn't need. I left my Goodwill book bag in the floor lounge with a note on it, and another retreatant discovered it as an answer to his prayers. Do we think God is not powerful enough to provide for us? Do you think you are not important enough for God to pay attention to your needs? Or have you gotten in the habit of giving yourself the credit when God answers your prayers? Ponder these questions, then read the passage a second time, slowly and prayerfully.

Oratio: Was there a time when it seemed like God didn't provide for you when a prayer went unanswered or a need unfulfilled? Have others let you down, making it easy to believe that God, too, will let you down? Listen to your heart and whatever fears, worries, or hurts are present there. Then speak to God honestly and openly about your concerns.

Contemplatio: Read the passage a third time. This time listen for how God answers your heart. God will earn your trust if you give him the chance. Will you give him the chance today? Spend some time with Jesus and his Father before moving on.

SUGGESTIONS FOR JOURNALING

1. The word, phrase, or idea that most spoke to me from today's passage was …
2. I have experienced God's providence when …
3. I want to trust God, but I am afraid that …
4. Jesus trusted his Father and wants me to do the same. What about the example of Jesus encourages me?
5. God doesn't stop responding just because we end our prayer time. Keep your eyes open for God's providence today and spend some time journaling in those moments at the end of today's prayer time or when you pray tomorrow.

282 *January 27 — Tuesday*

After you've journaled, close with a brief conversation thanking God for providing for your needs in today's prayer experience. Then pray an Our Father.

January 28 — Wednesday
Wednesday of the Third Week in Ordinary Time

ST. THOMAS AQUINAS, DOCTOR OF THE CHURCH, MEMORIAL

Born in 1225 to minor Italian nobility, Thomas's family intended for him to become abbot of the prestigious monastery of Monte Cassino in southern Italy. The monks sent him to the University of Naples for his theological studies. There he encountered the Order of Preachers (Dominicans), a new mendicant order that preached the Gospel, lived in poverty, and begged for their food. Against his family's strenuous objections, Thomas left the Benedictines and became a Dominican. He is considered one of the greatest philosophers and theologians of all time. The greatest irony was that his classmates, seeing that he was big and quiet, assumed he was quite stupid and gave him the nickname "The Dumb Ox." Perhaps God's plans for your life do not match up to what your family or classmates see in you.

Preparation: *Come, Holy Spirit, enlighten the eyes of my heart.* Be present to the God who is always present to you. Call to mind his loving care for you and spend the first minute of your prayer just resting in the free, unearned gift of loving and being loved. Let gratitude rise in your heart.

Set the Scene: Ask God for the grace to hear him calling you and to follow him faithfully in your daily life. At first glance, it appears that Jesus is trying to be alone to mourn the death of his cousin. However, Jesus' actions have symbolic value. Up until this point, he has been traveling from town to town and mostly preaching in synagogues. By moving to a deserted place, he is inviting them to seek him out. Those who seek him are rewarded. It also creates an opportunity of faith for Jesus' disciples. Will they trust in the Father, as Jesus does? Read the passage and picture the scene in your imagination.

MATTHEW 14:13-21

When Jesus heard of [the death of John the Baptist], he withdrew in a boat to a deserted place by himself. The crowds heard of this and followed him on foot from their towns. When he disembarked and saw the vast crowd, his heart was moved with pity for them, and he cured their sick. When it was evening, the disciples approached him and said, "This is a deserted place and it is already late; dismiss the crowds so that they can go to the villages and buy food for themselves." [Jesus] said to them, "There is no need for them to go away; give them some food yourselves." But they said to him, "Five loaves and two fish are all we have here." Then he said, "Bring them here to me," and he ordered the crowds to sit down on the grass. Taking the five loaves and the two fish, and looking up to heaven, he said the blessing, broke the loaves, and gave them to the disciples, who in turn gave them to the crowds. They all ate and were satisfied, and they picked up the fragments left over — twelve wicker baskets full. Those who ate were about five thousand men, not counting women and children.

Action! When God seems to withdraw, do you make the effort to seek him out? What do you do when your resources appear too small to meet the demands that are placed upon you? I know you've experienced the feeling of not enough time, not enough money, not enough knowledge or skill or talent. If you did some fasting for the unborn yesterday, you might have been reminded of the desperate craving that hunger brings. Jesus shows us what to do when we don't have enough: Take the little that we do have and give it to him. I experienced having not enough time to write this book. I gave it to God, and I had the time I needed to finish, as you can see by the fact that you are holding this book in your hands. What does each person experience in today's reading? Put yourself into the passage wherever you feel most comfortable — as a disciple or as one of the five thousand.

Acknowledge: Read the passage a second time. What are the thoughts, feelings, and desires that arise in your heart? What are you hungry for? Where do you feel inadequate?

Relate: Sit with Jesus on the grass and talk to him about it. Everyone else is busy eating or napping after the meal, so he has plenty of time to listen just to you.

Receive: Read the passage a third time. How does Jesus respond? What is he inviting you to?

Respond: Childlike trust is possible for all of us. It may look hard, but it's actually easier than the way you are already living your life. We have been taught not to trust and to make life more complicated than it was meant to be. Can you see yourself and the world as Jesus sees you? Can you do what Jesus asks you to do? Don't force yourself. Jesus reverences your freedom, and you should too. Enjoy Jesus' patient, gentle, loving presence with you for a few minutes before moving on.

SUGGESTIONS FOR JOURNALING
1. As I imagined the scene, what stood out to me was …
2. When have I felt inadequate?
3. Was there a time when I turned over my inadequacy to Jesus and he blessed me with more than enough?
4. In what area of my life is Jesus inviting me to greater trust?
5. I ended prayer with a sense that …

286 *January 28 — Wednesday*

After you've journaled, close with a brief conversation thanking God for his loving care for you experienced in today's prayer time. Then pray an Our Father.

January 29 — Thursday
Thursday of the Third Week in Ordinary Time

Preparation: *Come, Holy Spirit, enlighten the eyes of my heart.* Be present to the God who is always present to you. Call to mind his loving care for you and spend the first minute of your prayer just resting in the free, unearned gift of loving and being loved. Let gratitude rise in your heart.

Set the Scene: Ask God for the grace to hear him calling you and to follow him faithfully in your daily life. The Sea of Galilee is not excessively large. Extending thirteen miles north to south and seven miles east to west, most days an observer on one shore can easily see the opposite shore. Due to the interaction with surrounding arid land and the nearby Mediterranean Sea, violent squalls sometimes blow up. The disciples have literally been rowing all night. We know this because the Romans divided the night into four "watches," equal periods of time between sunset and sunrise. The "fourth watch" is the final three-hour period before sunrise. Read the passage and picture the scene in your imagination.

MATTHEW 14:22–33

Then he made the disciples get into the boat and precede him to the other side, while he dismissed the crowds. After doing so, he went up on the mountain by himself to pray. When it was evening he was there alone. Meanwhile the boat, already a few miles offshore, was being tossed about by the waves, for the wind was against it. During the fourth watch of the night, he came toward them, walking on the sea. When the disciples saw him walking on the sea they were terrified. "It is a ghost," they said, and they cried out in fear. At once [Jesus] spoke to them, "Take courage, it is I; do not be afraid." Peter said to him in reply, "Lord, if it is you, command me to come to you on the water." He said, "Come." Peter got out of the boat and began to walk on the water toward Jesus. But when he saw how [strong] the wind was he became frightened; and, beginning to sink, he cried out, "Lord, save me!" Immediately Jesus stretched out his hand and caught him, and said to him, "O you of little faith, why did you doubt?" After they got into the boat, the wind died down. Those who were in the boat did him homage, saying, "Truly, you are the Son of God."

Action! It's not so hard to imagine walking on water on a calm day, but would you attempt it when the waves are rolling? Peter did, and he was perfectly fine until he took his eyes off Jesus. As you play the scene forward in your mind, what most stands out to you?

Acknowledge: "Come!" Would you have the faith to get out of the boat? When have you felt like you were sinking? Did you call out to Jesus, "Lord, save me!" — or were you silent? Notice your thoughts and feelings that emerge as you read the passage a second time.

Relate: The winds have died down, and the sea is calm. Sit next to Jesus in the boat and talk to him about it.

Receive: Read the passage a third time. How does Jesus respond? What is in Jesus' heart for you?

Respond: Continue the conversation with the one who made you, and who knows you even better than you know yourself. See yourself, and your situation, through Jesus' eyes. Rest in his friendship for a few minutes before moving on.

SUGGESTIONS FOR JOURNALING
1. I feel like I've been rowing all night with the wind and the waves against me when ...
2. I felt like I was sinking when ...
3. Jesus calmed the storm in my heart when ...
4. Sitting in the boat next to Jesus makes me feel ...
5. I ended prayer with a burning desire for ...

After you've journaled, close with a brief conversation thanking God for the experience of his loving presence in today's prayer. Then pray an Our Father.

January 30 — Friday
Friday of the Third Week in Ordinary Time

Preparation: *Come, Holy Spirit, enlighten the eyes of my heart.* Be present to the God who is always present to you. Call to mind his loving care for you and spend the first minute of your prayer just resting in the free, unearned gift of loving and being loved. Let gratitude rise in your heart.

Lectio: Ask God for the grace to hear him calling you and to follow him faithfully in your daily life. The call to follow Jesus is not fundamentally a call to go somewhere or do something. It is a call to *be with Jesus* and to *learn from him*. We have been learning about Jesus' absolute trust in the Father. Now we realize that Jesus will trust the Father with his life even if it means death, death on the cross. His death means life for the whole world. Paradoxically, every Christian is called to become truly alive through a life of self-sacrifice. Ponder what you are called to as you read this passage today.

MATTHEW 16:21–27

From that time on, Jesus began to show his disciples that he must go to Jerusalem and suffer greatly from the elders, the chief priests, and the scribes, and be killed and on the third day be raised. Then Peter took him aside and began to rebuke him, "God forbid, Lord! No such thing shall ever happen to you." He turned and said to Peter, "Get behind me, Satan! You are an obstacle to me. You are thinking not as God does, but as human beings do."

Then Jesus said to his disciples, "Whoever wishes to come after me must deny himself, take up his cross, and follow me. For whoever wishes to save his life will lose it, but whoever loses his life for my sake will find it. What profit would there be for one to gain the whole world and forfeit his life? Or what can one give in exchange for his life? For the Son of Man will come with his angels in his Father's glory, and then he will repay everyone according to his conduct."

Meditatio: The Anointed One (*Messiah* in Hebrew, *Christos* in Greek) was supposed to be a descendant of King David. He would defeat the enemies of Israel and restore the trampled people to their former glory and rightful place in the world. Just before today's passage, Simon confessed that Jesus was the Messiah. Jesus called him blessed, renamed him "Peter" ("rock"), and promised him the keys to the kingdom of heaven (see Mt 16:13–20). Jesus then makes them promise not to tell anyone and begins to explain that the Messiah will suffer and die a miserable death for the sins of the people. God's ways are not our ways. Sometimes we think that following Jesus will make everything easy and take away all our problems, only to find that life has become harder instead of easier. Instinctively we know that self-sacrifice is the pinnacle of self-giving love. We admire it in others, but we struggle when it is our turn to live self-sacrificing love.

Oratio: How is Jesus calling you to a deeper faith in him, and to a deeper love for God and for others? What form does the cross take in your life right now? Read the passage a second time and notice what thoughts and feelings and desires emerge in your heart. Speak to Jesus with the same honesty as Peter. Don't be afraid of how Jesus might respond to you.

Contemplatio: Read the passage a third time and receive God's response to your prayers. Jesus didn't carry his cross alone (see Mt 27:32; Mk 15:21; Lk 23:26). Jesus doesn't expect any Christian to carry his cross alone either. The invitation is to stick with Jesus even when things get difficult. What does Jesus want to say to you? How will Jesus help you? Rest in his loving care for you and his desire that you experience the fullness of life and every good thing.

SUGGESTIONS FOR JOURNALING
1. The person I know who best exemplifies self-sacrificing love is ...
2. I laid down my life, picked up my cross, and experienced a

deeper sense of meaning and purpose when ...
3. Through Jesus' sacrifice on the cross, I have been given the gift of ...
4. What worry, fear, hurt, or anxiety is preventing me from living my life as an act of self-giving love?
5. Jesus was with me and wanted me to know ...

After you've journaled, close with a brief conversation thanking Jesus for his loving care for you in today's prayer experience. Then pray an Our Father.

January 31 — Saturday
Saturday of the Third Week in Ordinary Time

ST. JOHN BOSCO, MEMORIAL

REVIEW

Preparation: *Come, Holy Spirit, enlighten the eyes of my heart.* Call to mind God's loving care for you and spend the first minute of your prayer just resting in the free, unearned gift of loving and being loved.

What is it that you desire? Ask God in your own words for the desire of your heart.

This past week, we looked at the call of Jesus' disciples and the call that God has for your life. Review the past week's journal entries. As you do, notice what emerged in the conversation. Here are some questions to help you:

1. Where did I notice God, and what was he doing or saying?
2. How did I respond to what God was doing?
3. I felt God's love most strongly when …
4. I found myself struggling with …
5. I'm grateful for …
6. God seemed to be calling me or inviting me to …
7. This past week, my strongest sense, image, moment, or experience of God's loving presence was …

January 31 — Saturday

Conclude by conversing with God about your week. **Acknowledge** what you have been experiencing. **Relate** it to him. **Receive** what he wants to give you. **Respond** to him. Then savor that image of God's loving presence and rest there for a minute or two. Close with an Our Father.

Week Ten

A Light to the Nations

Welcome to the last two days of your *Oriens* pilgrimage. The feast of the Presentation commemorates the moment when Mary and Joseph brought baby Jesus to the Temple (see Lk 2:22–40). The law of Moses required the purification of a mother forty days after the birth of a male child (Lv 12:1–8). It also stipulated that the firstborn belonged to the priests. A firstborn cow, sheep, or goat would be sacrificed to God. Child sacrifice was forbidden, but a firstborn son still belonged to God. So he would be ransomed by a payment of money (Ex 13:11–16; Nm 18:13–16). This is a reference to the tenth plague in Egypt, the death of the firstborn, and perhaps to the sacrifice of Isaac (Gn 22:2–14).

Saint Luke loves the Temple (his Gospel begins and ends in the Temple, and his symbol is the ox, a sacrificial animal). The way he writes about this moment, Jesus isn't being redeemed but rather *presented*. The unseen God has been worshiped here for centuries. Now God himself, in the Person of Jesus, is visiting his own Temple. He comes in the humble form of a little baby. However, his visit does not go unseen. Simeon and Anna are symbols of the whole Old Testament. They have grown old waiting for God's promises to be fulfilled. And they have not been disappointed.

Simeon declares: "Now, Master, you may let your servant go / in peace, according to your word, / for my eyes have seen your salvation, / which you prepared in sight of all the peoples, / a light for revelation to the Gentiles, / and glory for your people Israel" (Lk 2:29–32). Remember how, back at the beginning of Advent, we were told to watch? These two old people are still watching. And they are rewarded with a vision of the Savior and Lord whom all the people are waiting for. Simeon and Anna perfectly symbolize what our *Oriens* pilgrimage is all about. God has opened the eyes of their hearts to see his presence and action in apparently ordinary moments. They recognize Jesus, the light of the world, and they begin to glow with his divine light. My prayer for every pilgrim is that, as you have been watching vigilantly all these weeks, the eyes of your heart have been enlightened by the light of faith. I pray that Christmastime has lit your heart on fire and that you, too, have begun to glow more brightly with God's divine light.

Grace of the Week: On this final week of the journey, we prepare ourselves for Candlemas, the feast of the Presentation. The liturgy that day will invite us, "Let us also, gathered together by the Holy Spirit, proceed to the house of God to encounter Christ. There we shall find him and recognize him in the breaking of the bread, until he comes again, revealed in glory." Ask God for the grace to recognize him in the breaking of the bread until he comes again in glory.

February 1 — Sunday
Fourth Sunday in Ordinary Time

Preparation: *Come, Holy Spirit, enlighten the eyes of my heart.* Be present to the God who is always present to you. Call to mind his loving care for you and spend the first minute of your prayer just resting in the free, unearned gift of loving and being loved. Let gratitude rise in your heart.

***Lectio*:** Ask God for the grace to recognize him in the breaking of the bread until he comes again in glory. Jesus begins his famous Sermon on the Mount with the Beatitudes. The word in Greek is *makarios*, which means "blessed" or "happy." Even today, after two millennia of Christianity, the gospel values are still shockingly countercultural. The world does not in any way cherish poverty, mourning, meekness, those who hunger, those who are merciful, those who are clean of heart, or the peacemakers. Those who live in this way can expect to face persecution. Far from being ironic, Jesus is inviting us to realize that these difficult experiences are a greater blessing than winning the lottery or your favorite football team going to the Super Bowl. Read the passage slowly and prayerfully with an open mind and heart.

MATTHEW 5:1–12A (LECTIONARY)
*When Jesus saw the crowds, he went up the mountain,
and after he had sat down, his disciples came to him.
He began to teach them, saying:
"Blessed are the poor in spirit,
for theirs is the kingdom of heaven.
Blessed are they who mourn,
for they will be comforted.
Blessed are the meek,
for they will inherit the land.
Blessed are they who hunger and thirst for righteousness,
for they will be satisfied.*

Blessed are the merciful,
for they will be shown mercy.
Blessed are the clean of heart,
for they will see God.
Blessed are the peacemakers,
for they will be called children of God.
Blessed are they who are persecuted for the sake of righteousness,
for theirs is the kingdom of heaven.
Blessed are you when they insult you and persecute you
and utter every kind of evil against you falsely because of me.
Rejoice and be glad,
for your reward will be great in heaven."

Meditatio: Imagine for a moment that the goal of human life is not to amass as much pleasure, power, prestige, or possessions as possible. Rather, human beings were made by love and for love. We are called to a life of self-giving love, which means to *love the Lord our God with all our heart, soul, mind, and strength,* and to *love others as Christ has loved us.* If love is our mission, then the circumstances that help us to truly be ourselves are a blessing. In other words, we are blessed when we are given the opportunity to more deeply love God and neighbor. Do you begin to see what Jesus is getting at? The objectively difficult experiences of our life are invitations to greater love. Ask the Holy Spirit to help you see your life from God's perspective.

Oratio: Who is it that most perfectly exemplifies these Beatitudes? Look closely and we will see that Jesus himself is poor in spirit (see 2 Cor 8:9); he mourns (Lk 19:41); he is meek (Mt 11:29); he hungers for righteousness (Mt 23:37); he is merciful (Lk 23:34); he is clean of heart (Heb 4:15); he is a peacemaker (Eph 2:14); and he is persecuted. The Beatitudes are like a portrait of Jesus. He is calling you to be like himself. Gaze at the face of Jesus and see his desire to richly bless you. Read the passage again and notice what moves your heart. Speak to him from your heart.

***Contemplatio*:** Read the passage a third time. This time receive whatever grace or blessing God desires to give you in this moment. Rest in his love for you with confidence and peace for a few minutes.

SUGGESTIONS FOR JOURNALING

1. The Beatitude that most "looks like Jesus" to me is …
2. The Beatitude that I most struggle to understand is …
3. I most desire the blessing of (pick one of the seven blessings Jesus names) …
4. Jesus is giving me, or inviting me to …
5. Today I will strive to live the Beatitudes more intentionally by …

304 *February 2 — Monday*

After you've journaled, close with a brief conversation thanking God for blessing you in today's prayer experience. Then pray an Our Father.

February 2 — Monday
Feast of the Presentation of the Lord

This feast commemorates the Presentation of the Child Jesus in the Temple forty days after his birth in Bethlehem. Traditionally on this day, the priest blesses the candles that will be used in church for the year. The faithful may also bring candles to be blessed that they will use in their homes. This is the final, formal conclusion to the Nativity of the Lord. The words of Simeon and the procession with candles now point us toward Lent and Easter.

Preparation: *Come, Holy Spirit, enlighten the eyes of my heart.* Be present to the God who is always present to you. Call to mind his loving care for you along your *Oriens* pilgrimage and spend the first minute of your prayer just resting in the free, unearned gift of loving and being loved. Let gratitude rise in your heart.

Set the Scene: Ask God for the grace to recognize him in the breaking of the bread until he comes again in glory. The Temple in Jerusalem is the largest and most impressive building most Jews have ever seen; it dominates the Jewish landscape — literally, politically, and religiously. The nation of Israel gathers here to worship the unseen, all-powerful God and to be cleansed of their sins. But there is something greater than the Temple here. God himself is entering his Temple, not with the fanfare of Palm Sunday, but borne in the arms of his virgin mother. Picture the contrast between the awe-inspiring Temple and the humble reality of God's presence. Read the passage slowly and prayerfully.

LUKE 2:22–40 (LECTIONARY)
*When the days were completed for their purification
according to the law of Moses,
Mary and Joseph took Jesus up to Jerusalem
to present him to the Lord,*

just as it is written in the law of the Lord,
Every male that opens the womb shall be consecrated to the Lord,
and to offer the sacrifice of
a pair of turtledoves or two young pigeons,
in accordance with the dictate in the law of the Lord.

Now there was a man in Jerusalem whose name was Simeon.
This man was righteous and devout,
awaiting the consolation of Israel,
and the Holy Spirit was upon him.
It had been revealed to him by the Holy Spirit
that he should not see death
before he had seen the Christ of the Lord.
He came in the Spirit into the temple;
and when the parents brought in the child Jesus
to perform the custom of the law in regard to him,
he took him into his arms and blessed God, saying:

"Now, Master, you may let your servant go
in peace, according to your word,
for my eyes have seen your salvation,
which you prepared in sight of all the peoples,
a light for revelation to the Gentiles,
and glory for your people Israel."

The child's father and mother were amazed at what was said about him;
and Simeon blessed them and said to Mary his mother,
"Behold, this child is destined
for the fall and rise of many in Israel,
and to be a sign that will be contradicted
— and you yourself a sword will pierce —
so that the thoughts of many hearts may be revealed."
There was also a prophetess, Anna,

the daughter of Phanuel, of the tribe of Asher.
She was advanced in years,
having lived seven years with her husband after her marriage,
and then as a widow until she was eighty-four.
She never left the temple,
but worshiped night and day with fasting and prayer.
And coming forward at that very time,
she gave thanks to God and spoke about the child
to all who were awaiting the redemption of Jerusalem.

When they had fulfilled all the prescriptions
of the law of the Lord,
they returned to Galilee, to their own town of Nazareth.
The child grew and became strong, filled with wisdom;
and the favor of God was upon him.

Action! God's entry into his Temple does not go unnoticed. Simeon and Anna symbolize all the Old Testament patriarchs and matriarchs who trusted in God's promises and waited for the fulfillment of God's plans. Though their eyes have probably grown dim with age, they see more clearly than the rest of the people, because they see with the eyes of their heart — hearts full of faith and love. They are a model for us. Faith allows them to see what others miss and to understand what God is doing even in the humble situations of everyday life. What is going on in the hearts of Simeon and Anna as they gaze at the Christ Child with love and gratitude? Where do you see God the Father and the Holy Spirit?

Acknowledge: Read the passage again and notice what speaks to you personally. How does your heart leap for joy? Ask Mary to let you hold her child. What does it feel like to hold God's son, and to know that he was born for you, and that he will die for you?

Relate: Speak to the Christ Child, heart to heart. Invite him into your heart.

Receive: Open your heart to receive all that God wants to give you. Read the passage again and try to receive what God wants to give you. Ultimately, God wants us to receive the gift of himself.

Respond: Jesus lives in the heart of every believer. You are the gift he most treasures. Let your heart enter into a deeper communion with his heart. Let him cast out your darkness and fill you with his pure and holy light. Savor his loving presence for a few minutes before moving on.

SUGGESTIONS FOR JOURNALING
1. I was surprised by ...
2. The part that most spoke to me was ...
3. The greatest gift God has given me on this pilgrimage was ...
4. I find the light of Christ shining more brightly ...
5. I ended prayer wanting ...

After you've journaled, close with a brief conversation giving thanks to God for his humble, loving presence. Then pray an Our Father.

The Presentation of the Lord (Candlemas)

AT THE MASS

The people gather in the chapel or another suitable place outside the church where the Mass will be celebrated. They carry unlighted candles. The priest and his ministers wear white vestments. While the candles are being lighted, this canticle may be sung: *Behold, our Lord will come with power, to enlighten the eyes of his servants, alleluia.* Then the priest introduces the Mass:

> Dear brethren (brothers and sisters),
> forty days have passed since we celebrated the joyful feast
> of the Nativity of the Lord.
> Today is the blessed day
> when Jesus was presented in the Temple by Mary and Joseph.
> Outwardly he was fulfilling the Law,
> but in reality he was coming to meet his believing people.
> Prompted by the Holy Spirit,
> Simeon and Anna came to the Temple.
> Enlightened by the same Spirit,
> they recognized the Lord
> and confessed him with exultation.
> So let us also, gathered together by the Holy Spirit,
> proceed to the house of God to encounter Christ.
> There we shall find him
> and recognize him in the breaking of the bread,
> until he comes again, revealed in glory.

Then he blesses the candles:

> Let us pray.
> O God, source and origin of all light,
> who on this day showed to the just man Simeon

the Light for revelation to the Gentiles,
we humbly ask that,
in answer to your people's prayers,
you may be pleased to sanctify with your blessing + these candles,
which we are eager to carry in praise of your name,
so that, treading the path of virtue,
we may reach that light which never fails.
Through Christ our Lord.

Or:

O God, true light, who create light eternal,
spreading it far and wide,
pour, we pray, into the hearts of the faithful
the brilliance of perpetual light,
so that all who are brightened in your holy temple
by the splendor of these candles
may happily reach the light of your glory.
Through Christ our Lord.

R: Amen.

Let us go in peace to meet the Lord.

Or:

Let us go forth in peace.

R: In the name of Christ. Amen.

Once a Pilgrim, Always a Pilgrim

Pilgrimages always seem to end abruptly. You strive to reach your destination, you struggle on the road, and it seems as though you'll never get there. Then you realize it's the final day, the final miles, and the place of pilgrimage is just over the next hill! You have made it to your destination. You bask in the feeling of success, promise to stay in touch with your fellow pilgrims, and struggle to explain to your family what has happened to you.

Then it is back to your old life. But the old life looks different now; the journey has changed you. You see yourself, God, and the world around you in a different light. Hopefully you, too, have become a light. Christmastime has lit your heart with the warmth and light of God's love. Keep tending your candle! Keep burning and glowing with the light of faith. Carry that light to the dark corners of the world so that the light of God's love will spread to every heart and home.

Review of Reviews

When you have a little time, flip back to the very first day of your pilgrimage, Sunday, November 27, and look at how it all began. Then take a journey through the nine Saturday review days (pages 43, 75, 108, 143, 172, 202, 229, 264, and 293). Notice what was coming up. Reflect on where you have been and how God has been with you on the journey. Notice how the journey has changed you.

SUGGESTIONS FOR JOURNALING
1. How did God meet me on the road?
2. There's so much! But the part that most spoke to me was …
3. God was telling me that …
4. I was able to let go of …
5. The deepest desire that has emerged in my heart was …
6. The greatest gift God has given me on this pilgrimage is …
7. In exchange, I found that God asked that I would give him the gift of …
8. If I was going to try to put into words my newfound relationship with God, I would describe it as …

Acknowledge what the pilgrimage meant to you. **Relate** it to God. **Receive** what he wants to give you. **Respond** to him. Then savor God's loving presence and rest there for a minute or two. Close with an Our Father.

The Journey Continues

I always tell pilgrims that they need to keep walking. Our journey is never done until we *come to the end of our pilgrimage and enter the presence of God.** Here are some suggestions for you to continue the journey:

- Buy a journal. At the end of each day, answer two questions: 1) Where did I see God today? 2) What was God doing? Use the ARRR prayer form to pray with your daily experiences and journal the fruits of your prayer (p. 269).
- On the following pages, I give you outlines for four different forms of prayer. You might even want to tear out those pages and keep them with your journal.
- Start praying with the daily Scripture readings. You can find each day's readings at usccb.org/bible/readings/. Depending on the reading, you can use *lectio divina* or imaginative prayer for your prayer each day (see the Prayer Outlines, pp. 321 and 323).
- Subscribe to a monthly missal. I have used Magnificat for years, and I find it very helpful. It includes prayer for morning and evening, the daily readings, and some reflections and additional prayers. There are many other monthly missals to choose from, and all of them will help you pray daily.
- Need more help journaling? Check out the Monk Manual at monkmanual.com. This resource provides reflection space and prompts for you on a daily, weekly, and monthly basis. It helps you live life with more reflection and purpose.
- Another great journal option is Every Sacred Sunday, which has readings and journal space for Sundays and holy days. Check it out at https://everysacredsunday.com.
- Subscribe to my homily podcast. Learn more at PilgrimPriest.us/podcast.
- OSV has a number of Bible study resources. Browse their

offerings at https://www.osvcatholicbookstore.com/topic/bibles-bible-studies.html. Consider not only participating in a Bible study, but actually leading one at your local church or in your home.
- Lent is coming up soon. Start reflecting and praying about a theme for Lent and how to live Lent more intentionally.
- Consider making a real, honest-to-goodness walking pilgrimage. My diocese hosts the Walk to Mary every year, a one-day walking pilgrimage. Learn more at walktomary.com. Check out my website for the article "A Step-by-Step Guide to Walking Pilgrimages."

*Antiphon 1, Monday Week II, Morning Prayer, in *The Liturgy of the Hours*, 4 vols. (International Commission on English in the Liturgy, 1974).

Prayer Outlines

LECTIO DIVINA

Lectio divina can be used with any passage from Scripture. The key is to use Scripture as a conversation starter for a deep, personal conversation with the God who inspired it. Don't rush each step; let them naturally unfold. Remember that the goal is spending quality time with the God who loves you. As you read, think, talk, and listen, you will learn to spend time with God like an old friend.

Preparation: *Come, Holy Spirit, enlighten the eyes of my heart.* Be present to the God who is always present to you. Call to mind his loving care for you and spend the first minute of your prayer just resting in the free, unearned gift of loving and being loved. Let gratitude rise in your heart.

Lectio: Ask God for whatever grace it is you desire to receive in today's prayer time. Read the passage through, slowly and prayerfully.

Meditatio: Turn it over in your mind. The ancients compared meditation to a cow chewing its cud. What was the cultural context? What did the author mean? Perhaps a particular word, phrase, or idea speaks to us. Perhaps it connects to a previous meditation or another Scripture passage. What are your feelings as you read the passage?

Oratio: Read the passage again. Prayer must be a conversation between persons. Turn to God and begin a conversation with him. Speak to him what is on your heart — your thoughts, feelings, fears, and desires.

Contemplatio: Read the passage a third time. Now just receive what is on God's heart — his thoughts, feelings, and desires. Spend some time receiving God's love and resting in it. Prayer is experiencing how our Father looks at us with love. Holiness is learning to live in his long, loving gaze every moment of our life.

SUGGESTIONS FOR JOURNALING

Journaling isn't an essential part of the prayer, but I find it helps me to deepen the experience when I put into words what was happening in my prayer time. You might find questions like these helpful, or you might make your own list of journal questions.

1. The part that most spoke to me was …
2. What I brought to the Lord was …
3. God gave me …
4. I received a new insight, understanding, or sense of myself …
5. Apply something from the passage to your own life. (For example, a passage about John the Baptist: Who pointed out Jesus to me? When did I point out Jesus to another person? What virtue of John the Baptist do I feel called to imitate?)

After you've journaled, close with a brief conversation giving thanks to God for the prayer time together. End with an Our Father or another favorite prayer.

Imaginative Prayer

Imaginative prayer helps us disconnect from this present moment to connect us with the deep reality of God's loving, invisible presence with us right now. The goal is not to build imaginary castles in the air, but to look into the Bible and, through it, encounter the God who was present in the moment when the biblical passage was written and is present here with you today. The imagination helps to break the ice and start the conversation as you spend quality time with God. It works best with Scriptures that have a lot of visual description or action to them.

Preparation: *Come, Holy Spirit, enlighten the eyes of my heart.* Be present to the God who is always present to you. Call to mind his loving care for you and spend the first minute of your prayer just resting in the free, unearned gift of loving and being loved. Let gratitude rise in your heart.

Set the Scene: Ask God for whatever grace it is you desire to receive in today's prayer time. Read the passage through and picture the scene in your mind. Choose the time of day and the scenery. Populate it with people dressed in period clothes. (Alternatively, you can picture the scene happening in your own city or neighborhood.)

Action! Play the scene forward in your mind. Notice how the participants react and what they are thinking and feeling. Notice where Jesus is and what he is doing. (You can also notice Mary, God the Father, the Holy Spirit, etc.). Place yourself in the scene.

Acknowledge: Read the passage a second time. What does this passage stir up in your mind and heart? Pay attention to your thoughts, feelings, and desires. Don't worry whether they are "correct," just notice them without any judgment.

Relate: As the scene is finished, spend some time in conversation with Jesus. You can walk with him, sit with him in the scene, or just be aware of his presence in your prayer space. Share your thoughts, feelings, desires, and fears, honestly and openly.

Receive: Read the passage a third time. How does God respond to what you have shared? What is in God's heart for you? Receiving isn't meant to be hard work. It is about relaxing into God's loving presence, focusing on him, and noticing what word, Scripture passage, feeling, or reminder might come.

Respond: This is a chance to deepen the conversation. Ask a question about what God seems to be saying or just say, "Thank you." And like a good friend, let yourself just enjoy God's company for a little while.

SUGGESTIONS FOR JOURNALING
1. Something in my life that connected with the story …
2. As the scene played out, what struck me was …
3. I talked to Jesus about …
4. I sensed he wanted me to know, or to give me, or remind me …
5. I left prayer with a new insight, understanding, or a call to a new way of thinking or acting …

After you've journaled, close with a brief conversation giving thanks to God for your prayer experience. Then pray an Our Father or another favorite prayer.

Relational Prayer (ARRR)

Relational prayer is a great way of praying with the experiences of everyday life. No matter what kinds of struggles or challenges you are facing, you can always pause and take a moment to give them to God. Here's how you do it:

Preparation: *Come, Holy Spirit, enlighten the eyes of my heart.* Be present to the God who is always present to you. Call to mind his loving care for you and spend the first minute of your prayer just resting in the free, unearned gift of loving and being loved. Let gratitude rise in your heart.

Acknowledge: Notice what is going on inside of you — your thoughts, feelings, and desires. If you are examining a recent event, try to fill in the blank, such as: "When that person did/said/acted that way, it made me feel __." There may be a number of different feelings that happened in quick succession. If your feelings are so strong they're making it hard to concentrate, pray the name of Jesus a few times and stick with the preparation period until you notice his peaceful presence. When the feeling is anger, try to notice what you were thinking and feeling just before you got angry. That can be a clue to where the anger came from and what God might want you to share with him. If you are feeling numb, or have no feelings at all, ask the Holy Spirit to help you connect with your feelings. We may need to give ourselves permission to feel our feelings.

Relate: Share with the Lord what is going on inside of you. Be honest with God. Sometimes we are mad at God himself because he appears to be ruining our lives or ignoring our prayers. You can get mad at God. Tell him how you feel, even if it includes inappropriate words. It's really important that we be completely honest. Do not try to ask God to give you something or do something at this stage. Just tell him what is going on with you.

Receive: Now we shift our attention from us and our problems to God. This is where I often got stuck when I was learning this prayer form.

Picture this scene: I'm struggling with something. A good friend comes and stands next to me. I point out the problem, tell him everything, and he listens patiently. God and I are looking at my problem together. Now, I turn to focus on my friend. What is in his heart for me? How does he look at me? It's his turn to talk. Sometimes it's just knowing that he cares, a feeling of peace, or that I am not alone in my problem. Sometimes it might be a Scripture passage or a few words to put me in my place or add perspective. Like with any good friend, it may not be exactly what I want to hear, but it will be what I need to hear.

Respond: If what he just gave you is hard to receive, tell him so. If it comforts you, thank him. Even if you don't get anything at this time, you can be confident that God will answer you when he is ready and will give you what you really need. So, keep your eyes and ears open in case he has more to say or give you later.

Sharing your burdens with God makes them melt like snow in the sunshine. It's almost like magic, but better. We call it *grace*. Practice this prayer time with the experiences of your everyday life.

SUGGESTIONS FOR JOURNALING

1. My strongest thought, feeling, or emotion was …
2. I needed to share with God that …
3. God wanted me to know …
4. In the course of my prayer time, I realized that …
5. I ended prayer with a new way of thinking, acting, responding, or believing …
6. I feel called by God to …

Feel free to journal whatever from the above struck you. Then spend a few minutes thanking God for the quality time together, and end with an Our Father or another favorite prayer.

The Saturday Review

I like to keep an old canning jar as a "gratitude jar." I start at New Year's, and each Saturday, I write on a slip of paper the one thing I am most grateful for that week and add it to the jar. At the end of the year, I dump out the jar and review my blessings. If you're interested in adopting this practice for yourself, a Saturday review like those we did throughout the *Oriens* pilgrimage can help fill your jar.

Preparation: *Come, Holy Spirit, enlighten the eyes of my heart.* Call to mind his loving care for you and spend the first minute of your prayer just resting in the free, unearned gift of loving and being loved. Let gratitude rise in your heart.

Flip back through your past week's journal entries. If you don't journal, cast your mind back through your week. Where did you go to Mass last Sunday? What did you receive from Mass? What was a high point this week? What was a low point? Here are some questions to help you:

1. My biggest blessing in the past week was …
2. My biggest challenge was …
3. Where did I notice God, and what was he doing or saying?
4. How did I respond to what God was doing?
5. I felt God's love most strongly when …
6. I'm grateful for …
7. This past week, my strongest sense, image, moment, or experience of God's loving presence was …

Journal for a little while whatever you are experiencing.

Conclude by conversing with God about your week. **Acknowledge** what you have been experiencing. **Relate** it to him. **Receive** what he wants to give you. **Respond** to him. Then savor that image of God's loving presence and rest there for a minute or two. Close with a Glory Be.

About the Author

Father Joel Sember was ordained a priest in 2007 for the Diocese of Green Bay, Wisconsin. He has extensive experience as a parish priest and two years of service in campus ministry. He made a thirty-day Ignatian silent retreat and later completed the Spiritual Direction Training Program through the Institute for Priestly Formation in Omaha, Nebraska. He holds a bachelor's in philosophy and Catholic studies from the University of St. Thomas, a bachelor's in sacred theology from the Pontifical Gregorian University, and a license in sacred theology from the Pontifical University Santa Croce in Rome. He has completed a dozen walking pilgrimages. He currently serves as pastor of four parishes in rural northeastern Wisconsin. Between ministry and parish meetings, he rides a motorcycle and paddles a kayak around great Wisconsin lakes. You can listen to his homily podcast every Sunday at PilgrimPriest.us.